DATE DUE

COMMUNITY

The Structure of Belonging

PETER BLOCK

BK

Berrett–Koehler Publishers, Inc.
San Francisco
a BK Business book

Berrett-Koehler Publishers, Inc.
235 Montgomery Street, Suite 650
San Francisco, CA 94104-2916
Tel: (415) 288-0260   Fax: (415) 362-2512   www.bkconnection.com

ORDERING INFORMATION

Quantity sales. Special discounts are available on quantity purchases by
corporations, associations, and others. For details, contact the "Special
Sales Department" at the Berrett-Koehler address above.
Individual sales. Berrett-Koehler publications are available through
most bookstores. They can also be ordered directly from Berrett-Koehler:
Tel: (800) 929-2929; Fax: (802) 864-7626; www.bkconnection.com
Orders for college textbook/course adoption use. Please contact Berrett-
Koehler: Tel: (800) 929-2929; Fax: (802) 864-7626.
Orders by U.S. trade bookstores and wholesalers. Please contact Ingram
Publisher Services, Tel: (800) 509-4887; Fax: (800) 838-1149; E-mail:
customer.service@ingrampublisherservices.com; or visit www.ingram
publisherservices.com/Ordering for details about electronic ordering.

Berrett-Koehler and the BK logo are registered trademarks of Berrett-
Koehler Publishers, Inc.

Printed in the United States of America

Berrett-Koehler books are printed on long-lasting acid-free paper. When it is
available, we choose paper that has been manufactured by environmentally
responsible processes. These may include using trees grown in sustainable
forests, incorporating recycled paper, minimizing chlorine in bleaching, or
recycling the energy produced at the paper mill.

Library of Congress Cataloging-in-Publication Data

Block, Peter.
    Community : the structure of belonging / Peter Block.
      p. cm.
    Includes bibliographical references and index.
    ISBN 978-1-57675-487-0 (hardcover)
    ISBN 978-1-60509-277-5 (pbk.)
    1. Communities. I. Title.
HM756.B56 2008
307—dc22   2007052814

FIRST EDITION

14 13 12 11 10   10 9 8 7 6 5 4 3

Developmental editor: Leslie Stephen
Production, interior design, and composition: Leigh McLellan Design
Copy editor: Elissa Rabellino
Cover designer: Bookwrights/Mayapriya Long

To Maggie

In appreciation for your commitment, intelligence, love, and integrity that make what I do possible. You are a placeholder for all who give their talents and love in support of others. Plus, you got the point of it all: You have chosen adventure over safety. This, in itself, is a rare gift.

Contents

Welcome   xi

INTRODUCTION   The Fragmented Community
and Its Transformation   1

Part One: The Fabric of Community

CHAPTER 1   Insights into Transformation   11

CHAPTER 2   Shifting the Context for Community   29

CHAPTER 3   The Stuck Community   37

CHAPTER 4   The Restorative Community   47

CHAPTER 5   Taking Back Our Projections   55

CHAPTER 6   What It Means to Be a Citizen   63

CHAPTER 7   The Transforming Community   73

Part Two: The Alchemy of Belonging

CHAPTER 8   Leadership Is Convening   85

CHAPTER 9   The Small Group Is the Unit of
Transformation   93

CHAPTER 10   Questions Are More Transforming
             Than Answers   101

             Midterm Review   111

CHAPTER 11   Invitation   113

CHAPTER 12   The Possibility, Ownership, Dissent,
             Commitment, and Gifts Conversations   123

CHAPTER 13   Bringing Hospitality into the World   145

CHAPTER 14   Designing Physical Space That
             Supports Community   151

CHAPTER 15   The End of Unnecessary Suffering   163

MORE   Book at a Glance   177

             Role Models and Resources   187

             Acknowledgments   223

             Index   227

             About the Author   237

             About the Design   239

The first human who hurled an insult
instead of a stone
was the founder of civilization.

Sigmund Freud

Welcome

This book is written to support those who care for the well-being of their community. It is for anyone who wants to be part of creating an organization, neighborhood, city, or country that works for all, and who has the faith and the energy to create such a place.

I am one of those people. Whenever I am in a neighborhood or small town and see empty storefronts, watch people floating aimlessly on the sidewalks during school or working hours, pass by housing projects, or read about crime, poverty, or a poor environment in the places where our children and our brothers and sisters live, I am distressed and anguished. It has become impossible for me to ignore the fact that the world we are creating does not come close to fulfilling its promise.

Along with this distress comes the knowledge that each of us, myself included, is participating in creating this world. If it is true that we are creating this world, then each of us has the power to heal its woundedness. This is not about guilt, it is about accountability. Citizens, in their capacity to come together and choose to be accountable, are our best shot at making a difference.

This book is for all who are willing to take a leadership role that affirms the conviction that without a willingness to be accountable for our part in creating a strong and connected community, our desire to reduce suffering and increase happiness in the world becomes infinitely more difficult to fulfill. It is also based on the belief that in some way the vitality and connectedness of our communities will determine the strength of our democracy.

• • •

Community as used here is about the experience of belonging. We are in community each time we find a place where we belong. The word *belong* has two meanings. First and foremost, to belong is to be related to and a part of something. It is membership, the experience of being at home in the broadest sense of the phrase. It is the opposite of thinking that wherever I am, I would be better off somewhere else. Or that I am still forever wandering, looking for that place where I belong. The opposite of belonging is to feel isolated and always (all ways) on the margin, an outsider. To belong is to know, even in the middle of the night, that I am among friends.

One goal in exploring the concepts and methods of community building in this book is to increase the amount of belonging or relatedness that exists in the world. Experiencing this kind of friendship, hospitality, conviviality is not easy or natural in the world we now live in.

The second meaning of the word *belong* has to do with being an owner: Something belongs to me. To belong to a community is to act as a creator and co-owner of that community. What I consider mine I will build and nurture. The work, then, is to seek in our communities a wider and deeper sense of emotional ownership; it means fostering among all of a community's citizens a sense of ownership and accountability.

Belonging can also be thought of as a longing to be. Being is our capacity to find our deeper purpose in all that we do. It is the capacity to be present, and to discover our authenticity and whole selves. This is often thought of as an individual capacity, but it is also a community capacity. Community is the container within which our longing to be is fulfilled. Without the connectedness of a community, we will continue to choose not to be. I have always been touched by the term *beloved community*. This is often expressed in a spiritual context, but it also is possible in the secular aspects of our everyday life.

My intent in this book is to give definition to ways of structuring the experience of belonging—that's why the first noun in its subtitle is *structure*. Belonging does not have to be left to chance or be dependent on the welcoming nature of others.

My thinking about structure has been shaped by a quote from a wonderful periodical devoted to art and architecture called *The Structurist:*

The word *structure* means to build, to construct, to form, as well as the organization or morphology of the elements involved in the process. It can be seen as the embodiment of creation . . . a quest not only for form but also for purpose, direction and continuity. [*See* Role Models and Resources.]

This quote refers to art, and we can apply the same thoughts to community. The promise of what follows is to provide structural ways to create the experience of belonging, not only in places where people come just to be together socially, but especially in places where we least expect it. These include all the places where people come together to get something done—our meetings, dialogues, conferences, planning processes, all those gatherings where we assemble to reflect on and decide the kind of future we want for ourselves.

I especially like the word *structure* because it stands in relief to our concern about style. To offer structures with the promise of creating community gives leaders relief from the common story that leadership is a set of personal qualities we are born with, develop, or try on like a new suit to see if they fit. The structures in this book—both the thinking and the practices—can be chosen and implemented regardless of personal style, or lack thereof. We can create structures of belonging even if we are introverted and do not like to make eye contact.

A disclaimer: If you believe that our communities are basically doing well and all that's needed is to continuously improve them, then this book is not going to make a lot of sense. Its sole purpose is to provide a path toward creating a future different from what we now have.

A word about the structure of the book. I have included a summary of each chapter at its beginning. I got the idea from Christopher Alexander's *Timeless Way of Building*. There he said that if you do not want to read the whole book or a whole chapter, just read the summaries and you will get the point. Also, the main points are summarized in outline form at the end, so if you do not want to read the chapter summaries, or the text, you can go to the Book at a Glance and really save some time.

The Fragmented Community and Its Transformation

The essential challenge is to transform the isolation and self-interest within our communities into connectedness and caring for the whole. The key is to identify how this transformation occurs. We begin by shifting our attention from the problems of community to the possibility of community. We also need to acknowledge that our wisdom about individual transformation is not enough when it comes to community transformation. So, one purpose here is to bring together our knowledge about the nature of collective transformation. A key insight in this pursuit is to accept the importance of social capital to the life of the community. This begins the effort to create a future distinct from the past.

• • •

The need to create a structure of belonging grows out of the isolated nature of our lives, our institutions, and our communities. The absence of belonging is so widespread that we might say we are living in an age of isolation, imitating the lament from early in the last century, when life was referred to as the age of anxiety. Ironically, we talk today of how small our world has become, with the shrinking effect of globalization, instant sharing of information, quick technology, workplaces that operate around the globe. Yet these do not necessarily create a sense of belonging. They provide connection, diverse information, an infinite range of opinion. But all this does not create the connection from which we can become grounded and experience the sense of safety that arises from a place where we are emotionally, spiritually, and psychologically a member.

Our isolation occurs because western culture, our individualistic narrative, the inward attention of our institutions and our professions, and the messages from our media all fragment us. We are broken into pieces.

One aspect of our fragmentation is the gaps between sectors of our cities and neighborhoods; businesses, schools, social service organizations, churches, government operate mostly in their own worlds. Each piece is working hard on its own purpose, but parallel effort added together does not make a community. Our communities are separated into silos; they are a collection of institutions and programs operating near one another but not overlapping or touching. This is important to understand because it is this dividedness that makes it so difficult to create a more positive or alternative future—especially in a culture that is much more interested in individuality and independence than in interdependence. The work is to overcome this fragmentation.

To create the sense that we are safe and among friends, especially those we have not yet met, is a particular challenge for our cities and rural towns. The dominant narrative about our cities is that they are unsafe and troubled. Those we label "homeless," or "ex-offenders," or "disabled," or "at risk" are the most visible people who struggle with belonging, but isolation and apartness is also a wider condition of modern life. This is as true in our gated communities and suburbs as in our urban centers.

There is a particular isolation in the spaciousness and comfort of our suburbs. In these neighborhoods we needed to invent the "play date" for our children. Interaction among kids must be scheduled, much like a business meeting. On Tuesday, a mom must call another mom and ask, "Can Alex play with Phil on Thursday, at our house, say about 4? I will call if we are running late. The play date should last until roughly 5:45, to give both children time to freshen up for the family get-together at dinner." A far cry from the day of kids walking home after school and casually seeing who they ran into.

The cost of our detachment and disconnection is not only our isolation, our loneliness, but also the fact that there are too many people in our communities whose gifts remain on the margin. Filling the need for belonging is not just a personal struggle for connection, but also a community problem, which is our primary concern in this book. The effects of the fragmentation of our communities show up in low voter turnout, the struggle to sustain volunteerism, and the large portion of the population who remain disengaged. The struggle is also the reality for the millions of people around the world who are part of today's diaspora—the growing number of displaced people unable to return to their homeland, living and raising their children in a permanent state of transition.

Communities That Work for All

Community offers the promise of belonging and calls for us to acknowledge our interdependence. To belong is to act as an investor, owner, and creator of this place. To be welcome, even if we are strangers. As if we came to the right place and are affirmed for that choice.

To feel a sense of belonging is important because it will lead us from conversations about safety and comfort to other conversations, such as our relatedness and willingness to provide hospitality and generosity. Hospitality is the welcoming of strangers, and generosity is an offer with no expectation of return. These are two elements that we want to nurture as we work to create, strengthen, and restore our communities. This will not occur in a culture dominated by isolation, and its correlate, fear.

● ● ●

It is not my intent here to journalistically describe what healthy communities look like and where they exist. This is well documented. We have the success stories from Savannah, Boston, Chicago, Portland—all those places where community well-being has been on the rise over time. We have the pockets of authentic community in showcase organizational cultures such as Harley-Davidson and AES.

There is no need for more benchmarking of where the world is working. The reason is partly that we have already heard all the stories, and partly—and more important—that narratives of success give us hope and places to visit, but do not build our community. Social fabric and successful communities elsewhere cannot be imported. What works somewhere else ends up as simply another program here, which might be useful but does not shift the fundamentals that we are after.

What is needed is an exploration of the exact way authentic community occurs. How is it transformed? What fundamental shifts are involved? Too little is understood about the creation and transformation of a collective. I want to explore a way of thinking that creates an opening for authentic communities to exist and details what each of us can do to make that happen. The essence is to take a step forward in our thinking and design about the ways that people in communities come together to produce something new for themselves. By thinking in terms of a structure of belonging, we begin to build the capacity to transform our communities into ones that work for all.

The challenge is to think broadly enough to have a theory and methodology that have the power to make a difference, and yet be simple and clear enough to be accessible to anyone who wants to make that difference. We need ideas from a variety of places and disciplines to deal with the complexity of community. Then, acting as if these ideas are true, we must translate them into embarrassingly simple and concrete acts.

This means a shift in thinking that gives us clues about collective possibility. The shift in thinking is the focus of Chapters 1 through 7. Following that, we come to methodology, which many of you may consider the heart of the book. But without the shift in thinking, methodology becomes technique and practice becomes imitation.

• • •

One key perspective is that to create a more positive and connected future for our communities, we must be willing to trade their problems for their possibilities. This trade is what is necessary to create a future for our cities and neighborhoods, organizations and institutions—a future that is distinct from the past. Which is the point.

To create an alternative future, we need to advance our understanding of the nature of communal or collective transformation. We know a good deal about individual transformation, but our understanding about the transformation of human systems, such as our workplaces, neighborhoods, and towns, is primitive at best, and too often naive in the belief that if enough individuals awaken, and become intentional and compassionate beings, the shift in community will follow.

A Future Distinct from the Past

The core question, then, is this: What is the means through which those of us who care about the whole community can create a future for ourselves. that is not just an improvement, but one of a different nature from what we now have?

The kind of future we are primarily interested in is the way in which communities—whether in the workplace or neighborhood, rural town or urban center—create a wider sense of belonging among their citizens.

This is why we are not focused on individual transformation in this book. Individual transformation is the more popular conversation, and the choice not to focus on it is because we have already learned that the transformation of large numbers of individuals does not result in the transformation of communities. If we continue to invest in individuals as the primary target of change, we will spend our primary energy on this and never fully invest in communities. In this way, individual transformation comes at the cost of community.

•   •   •

The fact that a sense of community has practical importance is probably best established in the work of Robert Putnam in his book *Bowling Alone.* He found that community health, educational achievement, local economic strength, and other measures of community well-being were dependent on the level of *social capital* that exists in a community.

Geography, history, great leadership, fine programs, economic advantage, or any other factors that we traditionally use to explain success made a marginal difference in the health of a community. A community's well-being simply had to do with the quality of the relationships, the cohesion that exists among its citizens. He calls this *social capital.*

Social capital is about acting on and valuing our interdependence and sense of belonging. It is the extent to which we extend hospitality and affection to one another. If Putnam is right, to improve the common measures of community health—economy, education, health, safety, the environment—we need to create a community where each citizen has the experience of being connected to those around them and knows that their safety and success are dependent on the success of all others.

This is an important insight for our cities. If you look beneath the surface of even our finest cities and neighborhoods, there is too much suffering. It took the broken levees of Hurricane Katrina to expose to the world the poverty and fragile lives in New Orleans.

A Brief Statement of the Need

I live in Cincinnati, Ohio, which like most of our urban centers can be seen as New Orleans without the flood. While it has abundant assets and irreplaceable qualities, it also has challenges that are impossible to ignore, try as we might. Wherever we live, we are never more than a short ride from neighborhoods that are wounded with disinvested buildings and populated by those who live on the margin. To not see the struggle of those on the margin, to think this is the best of all possible worlds or that we are doing fine, especially if our particular street or neighborhood is safe and prosperous, is to live with blinders on.

We choose to live with blinders for good reason. There is great attraction to the suburban, upscale rural life or to residing in "hot" places. We are constantly reminded of the allure of gated communities, quaint and prosperous small towns, nationally acclaimed golden cities. The streets we most frequently hear about in these areas are clean and busy with pedestrians, their housing a string of jewels, center city vital and alive, and neighborhoods the source of great pride.

These prosperous places, though, are only the partial story. Take it from Jim Keene, a very wise and successful public servant. He has brought his humanity and vision into the cauldron of building community as city manager for Berkeley and Tucson, and now works for an association to build the capacity of other city managers. Jim once said that for every city that prospers, there is another city nearby that is paying the price for that prosperity.

We know we have a shrinking middle class, a growing separation between the well off and the underclass. You cannot look closely at even the great cities in the world without seeing serious underemployment, poverty, homelessness, neighborhoods with empty buildings, deteriorating environment, youth hanging out on street corners day and night, and concerns about public safety.

We know about the dropout rates and deplorable conditions of our urban schools and the difficulty of achieving affordable health care for all. The list goes on. But this is not the point. The question here is not about the nature of the struggles; it is about the nature of the cure.

So the focus in this book is about community transformation; it is about both those communities and places that are paying the price *and* their more prosperous neighbors. For even in prosperous places, the idea and experience of community are elusive. If you look closely, you realize that the social fabric of our culture is more fragile than we imagine.

PART ONE

The Fabric of Community

The social fabric of community is formed from an expanding shared sense of belonging. It is shaped by the idea that only when we are connected and care for the well-being of the whole that a civil and democratic society is created. It is like the Bodhisattva belief that not one of us can enter Nirvana until all others have gone before us.

> What is extraordinary appears to us as a habit, the dawn a daily routine of nature.
>
> Abraham Joshua Heschel

What makes community building so complex is that it occurs in an infinite number of small steps, sometimes in quiet moments that we notice out of the corner of our eye. It calls for us to treat as important many things that we thought were incidental. An afterthought becomes the point; a comment made in passing defines who we are more than all that came before. If the artist is one who captures the nuance of experience, then this is whom each of us must become. The need to see through the eyes of the artist reflects the intimate nature of community, even if it is occurring among large groups of people.

The key to creating or transforming community, then, is to see the power in the small but important elements of being with others. The shift we seek needs to be embodied in each invitation we make, each relationship we encounter, and each meeting we attend. For at the most operational and practical level, after all the thinking about policy, strategy, mission, and milestones, it gets down to this: How are we going to be when we gather together?

What this means is that theory devolves down to these every-day questions out of which community is actually lived: Whom do I choose to invite into the room? What is the conversation that I both become and engage in with those people? And when there are more than two of us together at the same time, how do we create a communal structure that moves the action forward?

It is in these kinds of questions that accountability is chosen and care for the well-being of the whole is embodied. Individual transformation is not the point; weaving and strengthening the fabric of community is a collective effort and starts from a shift in our mindset about our connectedness.

CHAPTER 1

Insights into Transformation

Social fabric is created one room at a time. It is formed from small steps that ask "Who do we want in the room?" and "What is the new conversation that we want to occur?" In community building, we choose the people and the conversation that will produce the accountability to build relatedness, structure belonging, and move the action forward.

A series of core insights informs us how to answer these questions. These insights include ideas on focusing on gifts, on associational life, and on the way all transformation occurs through language. Also critical are insights about the context that governs the conversations and the willingness to speak into the future.

Two additional strands in the fabric of community explored here are the need for each small step to capture a quality of aliveness and the need for it to evolve in an organic way. There is an established method for accomplishing this aliveness that values all voices in the room, uses the small group even in large gatherings, and recognizes that accountability grows out of the act of cocreation. The essence of creating an alternative future comes from citizen-to-citizen engagement that focuses at each step on the well-being of the whole.

• • •

Major influences on the belief system underlying this methodology of communal transformation come from several disciplines and people whose work has been radical in many ways; their insights are foundational for our purposes. There are many others who inform us and are mentioned in this book, but these five touch the core: John McKnight, Werner Erhard, Robert Putnam, Christopher Alexander, and Peter Koestenbaum. The sixth collection of insights is from a group of wizards who have given life to large group methodologies—some of whom are Marvin Weisbord, Kathie Dannemiller, Dick and Emily Axelrod, Carolyn Lukensmeyer, Barbara Bunker, Billie Alban, and Juanita Brown.

There are two more people whose insights are important to understanding how the world changes. One is David Bornstein. His book *How to Change the World* analyzes nine social entrepreneurs who created large social movements around the globe. David's summary of why they were successful is worth our attention. Finally, I too briefly include the thinking of Allan Cohen. He translates the world of emergence and complex adaptive systems into language that once in a while I begin to think I understand.

I chose all of these people because I personally know most of them and they are the ones who have shaken my own thinking; their ideas have, for me, endured the test of time and experience.

What follows is a summary of the aspects of these people's work that are useful to this enterprise. I'll summarize their insights briefly and then weave them throughout the rest of the book.

The McKnight Insights:
Gifts, Associational Life, and Power

John McKnight is a leading light in the world of understanding the nature of community and what builds it. Three of his insights have permanently changed my thinking.

Focus on gifts. First and foremost, he asserts that community is built by focusing on people's gifts rather than their deficiencies. In the world of community and volunteerism, deficiencies have no market value; gifts are the point. Citizens in community want to know what you can do, not what you can't do.

In the professional world of service providers, whole industries have been built on people's deficiencies. Social service and most of medicine, therapy, and psychology are organized around what is missing or broken in people.

McKnight points out that if you go to a professional service provider and say you have no deficiencies or problems, that you just want to talk about your gifts and talents, you will be shown the door and treated as though you are wasting their time. Go to an association, or a group of neighbors, and tell them what your capabilities are, and they get quite interested.

This insight is profound if taken seriously, for it eliminates most of the conversations we now have about problem diagnosis, gap analysis (if you do not know what this is, be grateful), weaknesses, and what's wrong with me, you, and the rest of the world. It also underscores the limitation of labeling people. McKnight knows that the act of labeling, itself, is what diminishes the capacity of people to fulfill their potential. If we care about transformation, then we will stay focused on gifts, to such an extent that our work becomes to simply bring the gifts of those on the margin into the center.

John's focus on gifts has led to his founding a worldwide movement called Asset-Based Community Development. Simply put, this movement declares that if we want to make communities stronger, we should study their assets, resources, and talents. It is in the attention to these things that something new can occur.

Associational life. The second insight that is relevant here is about the limitations of systems. John sees a system as an organized group of funded and well-resourced professionals who operate in the domain of cases, clients, and services. As soon as you professionalize care, you have produced an oxymoron. He says that systems are capable of service but not care. Talk to any poor person or vulnerable person and they can give you a long list of the services they have received. They are well serviced, but you often have to ask what in their life has fundamentally changed.

The alternative to a "system" is what John calls "associational life": groups of people voluntarily coming together to do some good. In the disabilities world, John's work has been enthusiastically received. This has led to a widespread effort to take people with visible disabilities out of institutions and systems and bring them back into neighborhoods. Support groups are created, slowly, voluntarily, with a lot of phone calls and requests, so that ordinary citizens come together to support their new neighbors. This strategy brings generosity back into a neighborhood, and in the doing, citizens whose disabilities are hidden (all of us) experience a transformation in their own lives.

Power in our hands. The third insight for community building is John's faith in citizens to identify and solve problems for themselves. He finds that most sustainable improvements in community occur when citizens discover their own power to act. Whatever the symptom—drugs, deteriorating houses, poor economy, displacement, violence—it is when citizens stop waiting for professionals or elected leadership to do something, and decide they can reclaim what they have delegated to others, that things really happen. This act of power is present in most stories of lasting community improvement and change.

To summarize these insights from the work of John McKnight and his partner, Jody Kretzmann: Communities are built from the assets and gifts of their citizens, not from the citizens' needs or deficiencies. Organized, professionalized systems are capable of delivering services, but only associational life is capable of delivering care. Sustainable transformation is constructed in those places where citizens choose to come together to produce a desired future.

The Erhard Insights:
The Power of Language, Context, and Possibility

For over 30 years, Werner Erhard has created thinking and learning experiences that have affected millions of people's lives. Many of the ideas he has worked with derive from the work of others, but Werner has named and integrated them into something more powerful than where the thinking began. His work lives through the Landmark Corporation and other licensees. What I want to select from his work here is a small part of his legacy, but these are the ideas that have changed my practice.

The power of language. Werner understands the primal creative nature of language. Many of us have focused for years on improving conversations. We have known that dialogue and communication are important tools for improvement. Werner takes it to a whole new realm by asserting that all transformation is linguistic.

He believes that a shift in speaking and listening is the essence of transformation. If we have any desire to create an alternative future, it is only going to happen through a shift in our language. If we want a change in culture, for example, the work is to change the conversation—or, more precisely, to have a conversation that we have not had before, one that has the power to create something new in the world. This insight forces us to question the value of our stories, the positions we take, our love of the past, and our way of being in the world.

The power of context. Another insight is in the statement, "The context is decisive." This means that the way we function is powerfully impacted by our worldview, or the way, in his language, "the world shows up for us." Nothing in our doing or the way we go through life will shift until we can question, and then choose once again, the basic set of beliefs—some call it mental models; we're calling it context here—that lie behind our actions. Quoting Werner, "Contexts are constituted in language, so we do have something to say about the contexts that limit and shape our actions."

Implied in this insight is that we have a choice over the context within which we live. Plus, as an added bargain, we can choose a context that better suits who we are now without the usual requirements of years of inner work, a life-threatening crisis, finding a new relationship, or going back to school (the most common transformational technologies of choice).

The way this happens (made too simple here) is by changing our relationship with our past. We do this by realizing, through a process of reflection and rethinking, how we have not completed our past and unintentionally keep bringing it into the future. The shift happens when we pay close attention to the constraints of our listening and accept the fact that our stories are our limitation. This ultimately creates an opening for a new future to occur.

The power of possibility. Changing our relationships with our past leads to another aspect of language that Werner has carefully developed. This is an understanding of the potential in the concept and use of *possibility*. Possibility as used here is distinguished from other words like *vision, goals,* *purpose*, and *destiny*. Each of those has its own profound meaning, but all are different from the way Werner uses the word *possibility*. Possibility, here, is a declaration, a declaration of what we create in the world each time we show up. It is a condition, or value, that we want to occur in the world, such as peace, inclusion, relatedness, reconciliation. A possibility is brought into being in the act of declaring it.

For example, peace may not reign at this moment, but the possibility of peace does enter the room just because we have walked in the door. Peace here is a future not dependent on achievement; it is a possibility. The possibility is created by our declaration, and then, thankfully, it begins to work on us. The breakthrough is that we become that possibility, and this is what is transforming. The catch is that possibility can work on us only when we have come to terms with our story. Whatever we hold as our story, which is our version of the past, and from which we take our identity, becomes the limitation to living into a new possibility.

Werner has described this with more precision in recent personal correspondence:

> I suggest that you consider making it clear that it is the future that one lives into that shapes one's being and action in the present. And, the reason that it appears that it is the past that shapes one's being and action in the present is that for most people the past lives in (shapes) their view of the future.
>
> . . . it's only by completing the past (being complete with the past) such that it no longer shapes one's being and action in the present that there is room to create a new future (one not shaped by the past—a future that wasn't going to happen anyhow). Futures not shaped by the past (i.e., a future that wasn't going to happen anyhow) are constituted in language.
>
> In summary, (1) one gets complete with the past, which takes it out of the future (being complete with the past is not to forget the past); (2) in the room that is now available in the future when one's being and action are no longer shaped by the past, one creates a future (a future that moves, touches, and inspires one); (3) that future starts to shape one's being and actions in the present so that they are consistent with realizing that future.

Werner Erhard's way of thinking about language, context, and possibility are key elements in any thinking about authentic transformation. As with the other insights here, they are about a way of being in the world first, and then they can be embodied in concrete actions.

The Putnam Insights:
Social Capital and the Well-Being of Community

Robert Putnam wrote *Bowling Alone* and amplified the conversation about the role that social capital plays in building community. As one part of his extensive research, he studied a fair number of Italian towns and tried to understand why some were more democratic, were more economically successful, had better health, and experienced better education achievement.

His findings were startling, for he discovered that the one thing that distinguished the more successful from the less successful towns was the extent of social capital, or widespread relatedness that existed among its citizens. Success as a town was not dependent on the town's geography, history, economic base, cultural inheritance, or financial resources.

Putnam shows how we have become increasingly disconnected from family, friends, neighbors, and our democratic structures—and how we may reconnect. He warns that our stock of social capital—the very fabric of our connections with each other—has plummeted, impoverishing our lives and communities.

Geography, history, great leadership, fine programs, economic advantage, and any other factors that we traditionally use to explain success made a marginal difference in the health of a community. Community well-being simply had to do with the quality of the relationships, the cohesion that exists among its citizens. He calls this *social capital.*

In the book *Better Together,* Putnam and coauthor Lewis M. Feldstein explain that "*social capital* refers to social networks, norms of reciprocity, mutual assistance, and trustworthiness. The central insight of this approach is that social networks have real value both for the people in those networks . . . as well as for bystanders. Criminologists, for instance, have shown that the crime rate in a neighborhood is lowered when neighbors know one another well, benefiting even residents who are not themselves involved in neighborhood activities."

They go on to distinguish between "bonding" and "bridging" social capital. Bonding social capital are networks that are inward looking, composed of people of like mind. Other social networks "encompass different types of people and tend to be outward looking—bridging social capital." It is primarily the bridging social capital that we are interested in here. As Putnam and Feldstein put it: "[A] society that has *only* bonding social capital will . . . [be] segregated into mutually hostile camps. So a pluralistic democracy requires lots of bridging social capital, not just the bonding variety."

The Alexander Insights: Aliveness, Wholeness, and Unfolding

Christopher Alexander speaks from the world of architecture, but his thinking applies equally well to the creation of community. He grieves over the fragmented and mechanistic way we currently operate. In *The Nature of Order, Book 1: The Phenomenon of Life*, he writes,

> In discussing what to do in a particular part of a town, one person thinks poverty is the most important thing. Another person thinks ecology is the most important thing. Another person takes traffic as his point of departure. Another person views the maximization of profit from development as the guiding factor. All these points of view are understood to be individual, legitimate, and inherently in conflict. It is assumed that there is not a unitary view through which these many realities can be combined. They simply get slugged out in the marketplace, or in the public forum.
>
> But instead of lucid insight, instead of growing communal awareness of what should be done in a building, or in a park, even on a tiny bench—in short, of what is good—the situation remains one in which several dissimilar and incompatible points of view are at war in some poorly understood balancing act. [See Role Models and Resources.]

Aliveness and wholeness. The alternative to this fragmentation is to create structures that are defined by what Alexander calls "a quality of aliveness." The absence or presence of this quality has profound impact on the experience of being in that structure. Also, that quality of aliveness must be present in each step in the design and creation of the structure, for it to be present in the final product.

This aliveness grows out of a sense of wholeness. Wholeness is made up of a collection of separate centers, where each center has "a certain life or intensity. . . . We can see that the life of any one center depends on the life of other centers. This life or intensity is not inherent in the center by itself, but is a function of the whole configuration in which the center occurs."

To connect this to our discussion, we must ask whether every single step in our work holds this quality of life or intensity. Whether we're talking about a strategy, program, invitation, dialogue, gathering, or building a master plan, the human experience of aliveness in each choice or step has as much significance as any technical, economic, or purely practical consideration.

This aliveness also is most often found in surprising places. Often in irregular structures, all with aspects of imperfection. Alexander identifies 15 properties that create the wholeness and aliveness. It would take us off track to list them all here, but some are clearly to the point. Listen to the language he uses and you get a feel for the world he is naming: Deep Interlock and Ambiguity, Contrast, Roughness, Simplicity and Inner Calm, Not-Separateness.

It is easy to take these words, which he uses to reflect qualities in nature and in a room or building, and apply them to the world of social capital, human relatedness, and belonging that we are concerned with here. Much of what follows in the book is just this: bringing aliveness and wholeness to our notions of leadership, citizenship, social structures, and context, which are essential in creating the community of belonging and restoration that we desire.

Transformation as unfolding. One more influence from Alexander is his belief that aliveness and wholeness can occur only through a process of "unfolding." Transformation unfolds and is given structure by a consciousness of the whole. The task of transformation is to operate so that what we create grows organically, more concerned with the "quality of aliveness" that gives us the experience of wholeness than with a predictable destination and the speed with which we can reach it.

An unfolding strategy requires giving an uncomfortable importance to each small step we take. We have to worry as much about the arrangement of a room as we do about the community issue that caused us to assemble. It leads us to value the details of each step so that it becomes its own center. For example, each step of a master plan has to be a small example of the qualities we want in the final large thing. Throughout this book, you will see the effort to value the importance of small things; this intention is a direct outgrowth of Alexander's insights.

In summary, Christopher Alexander moves us toward aliveness, embodied in those places and moments that give us the experience of belonging. In the absence of aliveness, we unknowingly experience an inner conflict, a feeling of something unresolved.

The Koestenbaum Insights: Paradox, Freedom, and Accountability

For several decades, Peter Koestenbaum has brought the insights of philosophy to the business marketplace. His work on the Leadership Diamond is a holistic and practical landscape of what is required of leaders to achieve greatness in the world, both personally and for their institutions.

Appreciating paradox. One insight that informs our exploration of communal transformation is Peter's understanding of how we can come to terms with the paradoxical nature of human affairs. He values ambiguity and anxiety as the natural condition of being human. The painful choices people make in their lives and for their institutions are an affirming aspect of their humanity. These choices are not the sign of a problem, or weakness, or the world gone wrong. It is out of the subjectivity and complexity of life that transformation emerges. As a philosopher and consultant, Peter has always given voice to how profound the right question can be.

It is the willingness to reframe, turn, and even invert a question that creates the depth and opening for authentic change. Questions take on an almost sacred dimension when they are valued for their own sake. This is in stark contrast to the common need for answers and quick formulaic action.

Choosing freedom and accountability. A second thread that courses through this book, and also that has given coherence to all of Peter's work, is the search for human freedom—freedom being the choice to be a creator of our own experience and accept the unbearable responsibility that goes with that. Out of this insight grows the idea that perhaps the real task of leadership is to confront people with their freedom. This may be the ultimate act of love that is called for from those who hold power over others.

Choosing our freedom is also the source of our willingness to choose to be accountable. The insight is that freedom is what creates accountability. Freedom is not an escape from accountability, as the popular culture so often misunderstands.

One more way that Peter's work has formed my thinking about community is the idea that our willingness to care for the well-being of the whole occurs when we are confronted with our freedom, and when we choose to accept and act on that freedom.

The Insights of Large Group Methodology: Designing for the Experience of Community

Over the last 20 years, a rather small group of people has become quite sophisticated in bringing large groups of people together (from 50 to 5,000 at a time) to create visions, build strategy, define work processes, and create direction for institutions and communities. This body of knowledge has many names but is generally called *large group methodology*. While it is well established among expert practitioners, it has not found its way into the mainstream of how most leaders do planning and bring people together. These methods tend to be relegated to something that is pulled out on special occasions for special events. We treat these methods like sterling silver and use the stainless every day. This is a shame, for the difference between this kind of practice and the conventional way we bring people together is more like the difference between using sterling silver and eating with our hands.

These large group methods are too profound and too important to stay primarily in the hands of specialized experts. They need to be in the regular practice of community and institutional leaders. They are more than simply tools; they are the means of creating the experience of democracy and high engagement, which we say we believe in but rarely embody. As this thinking and practice grow, they have the potential to fundamentally change the nature of leadership, which would be a good thing.

Four of the innovators whose work is highlighted have been friends and teachers of mine for years. I reflect their thinking here only because I have been in many rooms with them. There are many others who have also changed the world and our thinking about bringing large groups of people together: Harrison Owen, Barbara Bunker, Billie Alban, Fred and Marilyn Emory, and Carolyn Lukensmeyer come to mind.

Future Search. Marvin Weisbord has created Future Search with Sandra Janoff. This structure begins with a scan of the environment and brings people into a conversation about the future they want to create. Marvin and Sandra have long understood the importance of the right question, the way to balance expert input with communal dialogue, and how to structure the flow of small group discussions into a collective outcome. They have also codified the distinction between solving problems and creating a future.

Conference Model. Dick and Emily Axelrod are design geniuses. They realized early on that if we can change the way we meet, we can change the way we live together. They know that learning best occurs when we structure meetings in a way that puts people in contact with each other where they experience in a conference the same dilemmas they face in life. They create experiences that simulate the democratic, self-governing principles that, if taken seriously, can create large communities of committed and powerful people.

Whole-Scale Change. The late Kathie Dannemiller was another innovator in this movement. "One heart—one mind" was the spirit that she lived, and her goal was to bring that into an event where people assembled to create a new future. She had a faith in the collective capacity of employees and citizens that would put Thomas Jefferson to shame.

Her guiding question was "How will the world be different tomorrow as a result of our meeting today?" Like the others, she valued the question and held deep skepticism about answers. She also knew that the questions with the most power were the ones that touched the heart and spoke to what people were experiencing. If "What did you know and when did you know it?" defined the Watergate hearings, the question "What did you hear and how did you feel about that?" was at the core of her work.

Kathie wanted the whole system in the room, and then she constantly broke it into small groups. She advocated that the small group worked best when it was maximally diverse—meaning that each small group was a microcosm of the large system. This composition plus a broad enough question results in people momentarily putting aside their own individual interests and beginning to care for the well-being of the whole.

The World Café. Finally, I want to talk of the work of Juanita Brown and her partner, David Isaacs. Their structure is called the World Café. Its gift is in its sophisticated simplicity. They begin by defining a large question that gets at the purpose of the gathering. Each small group focuses on the question, but in the Café method, the group sits at a round cocktail-sized table.

On that table is a flip chart sheet or butcher paper and a marker for each person. As people talk, each writes on the paper in large letters the ideas worth retaining. At certain intervals, as in musical chairs (except there are enough seats for all), one person stays as host at the table and the others go to different tables. The host summarizes for the new group what is on the paper, and the discussion continues. Eventually, the ideas from the tables are shared with the whole group. It is an elegant model to create convergence for a large group.

The Key Insights of Large Group Methodologies

Now, the intent here is not to describe the full process for any of these large group innovative methods—I know that I do each a great injustice in my minimalist descriptions and acknowledgment. The intent is to define some of the essential elements that form the design basis from this large group work that informs our thinking about community transformation.

Each element of each large group method has profound implications for how people meet, how they create an alternative future, and how community can be developed in a sustainable way. What we may once have relegated as useful but incidental little "training exercises" now have a power beyond our imagination. They form a way of thinking and operating in community that, when matched with the philosophical insights of the others, give us the structure of belonging that we seek. Here is a brief summary of the power of their thinking:

Accountability and commitment. The essential insight is that people will be accountable and committed to what they have a hand in creating. This insight extends to the belief that whatever the world demands of us, the people most involved have the collective wisdom to meet the requirements of that demand. And if we can get them together in the room, in the right context and with a few simple ground rules, the wisdom to create a future or solve a problem is almost always in the room. All you need to ensure this is to make sure the people in the room are a diverse and textured sample of the larger world you want to affect.

This insight is an argument for collective intelligence and an argument against expensive studies and specialized expertise. That is why this thinking finds a skeptical ear from the academy, most expert consultants, and the leadership that espouses democracy but really only trusts patriarchy and cosmetic empowerment.

Learning from one another. The key to gathering citizens, leaders, and stakeholders is to create in the room a living example of how I want the future to be. Then there is nothing to wait for, because the future begins to show up as we gather. One of the principles is that all voices need to be heard, but not necessarily all at one time or by everybody. What makes this succeed is that most everything important happens in a small group. Which expresses another principle, that peer-to-peer interaction is where most learning takes place; it is the fertile earth out of which something new is produced. In this small group you place the maximum mix of people's stories, values, and viewpoints, and in this way each group of 6 to 12 brings the whole system into that space.

Bias toward the future. The insights from large group methods have a bias toward the future and devote little or no time to negotiating the past or emphasizing those areas where we will never agree anyway. The most organizing conversation starter is "What do we want to create together?" So much for in-depth diagnoses, more studies, argument and negotiation, and waiting for the sponsorship or transformation of top leaders.

How we engage matters. The most important contribution of those who have developed these principles and insights is the idea that the way we bring people together matters more than our usual concerns about the content of what we present to people. How we structure the gathering is as worthy of attention as grasping the nature of a problem or focusing on the solutions that we seek.

The gift to us from these masters of large group work is the belief that transformation hinges on changing the structure of how we engage each other. It is the insight that authentic transformation does not occur by focusing on changing individuals or being smart about political processes, which are based on advocacy of interests, hardball negotiation, or finding where the power resides and getting them on your side. The insights of these masters are a dramatic shift from much of our conventional thinking, which, by the way, is not working that well.

The Bornstein-Cohen Insights: Scale, Speed, and Emergent Design

David Bornstein is a journalist who has written about the Grameen Bank in Bangladesh and other social innovations that have become large movements. Within the stories he tells in his books are some radical thoughts about how successful transformations came into being.

Small scale, slow growth. Not one of the examples David describes began as a government or large-system-sponsored program. Each was begun with very little funding, no fanfare, and little concern about how to measure the outcomes. Each had a deeply committed and self-chosen leader with a commitment to make a difference in the lives of however many people they were able to reach.

Bornstein concluded that well-funded efforts, with clear outcomes, that spell out the steps to get there do not work. Changes that begin on a large scale, are initiated or imposed from the top, and are driven to produce quick wins inevitably produce few lasting results. This may be a clue to why our wars such as those on drugs and poverty have been consistently disappointing and sometimes have even produced more of what they sought to eliminate.

If you reflect on the stories of the successful leaders who Bornstein documents, you realize that these entrepreneurs were committed enough and patient enough to give their projects time to evolve and find their own way of operating. There were years spent simply learning what structures, agreements, leadership, and types of people were required to be successful.

It was after the model had evolved and succeeded on its own terms that it began to grow, gain attention, and achieve a level of scale that touched large numbers of people.

This means that sustainable changes in community occur locally on a small scale, happen slowly, and are initiated at a grassroots level.

Emergent design. Allan Cohen is a brilliant strategy consultant who combines a deep understanding of the power of conversation with insights about the organic nature of design. A winning combination. Allan makes even more intentional and explicit the strategies that Bornstein has documented. Allan distinguishes between emergent strategies and destination or blueprint strategies. He says that effective change strategies obviously begin with a strong sense of purpose plus a commitment to bring something new into the world.

The key is what you do after that. He talks of two things: One is recognizing that organizations are always adapting and learning, even in the absence of big change initiatives. So a good place to start is by asking why the organization hasn't been moving naturally in a more desirable direction. Then take modest steps to impact the conversations and relationships that are shaping the direction of change inherent in the organization. Watch what emerges, pause, reflect, and course correct—then watch what emerges again. This is a crude definition of emergence.

A second insight from Allan is about changing the conditions under which an intention is acted upon. He claims the ability to herd cats, which many have said is impossible. He does this by tilting the floor, which changes the conditions under which the cats are operating. Emergent strategies focus on conditions more than on behaviors or predictable goals. Ironically, the act of predicting the path may be the obstacle to achieving the purpose.

Allan's work on emergent design places important emphasis on becoming clear on the purpose, the key to which is opening wide the possibility for a different future. He also gives importance to relatedness being the foundation of all achievement.

Combining the Insights

David Bornstein's stories are an expression of all the insights summarized here and woven throughout this book. For example, the efforts he talks about demonstrate the conditions leading to Alexander's quality of aliveness. They unfolded slowly and with great consciousness; then they became small whole centers in and of themselves, which finally, organically, began to combine with other centers to achieve some scale.

These efforts also had leaders who chose to live into Werner Erhard's concept of possibility. The ends seemed unachievable and the commitment was not contingent on results. Each project created a new conversation about the people involved. Take Grameen Bank as an example. The founder declared that poor people were creditworthy and excellent entrepreneurs. This was simply a declaration of possibility and began a new conversation about poverty that shifted the context within which loans were made.

By this shift in context, Muhammad Yunus, founder of Grameen, embodied McKnight's observation that development is based on gifts, not deficiencies.

Grameen Bank also counted on the power of community and relatedness. Yunus and his bank created teams of borrowers (they called them *chapters*), in which each person's ability to receive a loan was dependent on the repayment by others in the group. A portion of each repayment went to fund the loans to other chapters and the well-being of the community. These small groups were the basic unit of borrowing, four women to a group.

Not individuals, but the small group. Each small group also was required to operate as part of a larger community, so that they could not become insular and act as if the boundary of their group was the edge of the earth. This is the essence of the large group methodologies.

There was for each team of borrowers a set of requirements that went beyond the money. They were accountable for producing a successful life for themselves and others, which is a correlate of Koestenbaum's understanding of freedom—that freedom and accountability are one and the same.

And all of this resulted in the wider benefits of having created social capital, as Putnam would term it. The participation of the women in the entrepreneurial venture affected all aspects of their lives and that of their village. Eventually it would impact a nation.

So in this brief snapshot we have the core elements of the methods of collective transformation that follow. Integrating these insights gives us some basic conceptual elements for transforming communities. The reason to keep reading is to give more form and depth to these ideas and apply them to our world, however large or small we may define it.

CHAPTER 2

Shifting the Context
for Community

The context that restores community is one of possibility,
generosity, and gifts, rather than one of problem solving, fear, and
retribution. A new context acknowledges that we have all the capacity,
expertise, and resources that an alternative future requires. Communities are human systems given form by conversations that build relatedness. The conversations that build relatedness most often occur through
associational life, where citizens show up by choice, and rarely in the
context of system life, where citizens show up out of obligation. The
small group is the unit of transformation and the container for the experience of belonging. Conversations that focus on stories about the past
become a limitation to community; ones that are teaching parables and
focus on the future restore community.

• • •

Community occurs in part as a shift in context, the mental
models we bring to our collective efforts. It is a new context that
gives greater impact to the ways we work to make our communities better.
Context is the set of beliefs, at times ones that we are unaware of, that dictate how we think, how we frame the world, what we pay attention to, and
consequently how we behave. It is sometimes called a *worldview.*

The following are the shift in context that would signal a transformation
into authentic community:

- We are a community of possibilities, not a community of problems.

- Community exists for the sake of belonging and takes its identity from the gifts, generosity, and accountability of its citizens. It is not defined by its fears, its isolation, or its penchant for retribution.

- We currently have all the capacity, expertise, programs, leaders, regulations, and wealth required to end unnecessary suffering and create an alternative future.

Community is fundamentally an interdependent human system given form by the conversation it holds with itself. The history, buildings, economy, infrastructure, and culture are products of the conversations and social fabric of any community. The built and cultural environments are secondary gains of how we choose to be together.

Principles of Strategy

This context leads to certain principles of a strategy for community transformation:

- **The essential work is to build social fabric, both for its own sake and to enable chosen accountability among citizens.** When citizens care for each other, they become accountable to each other. Care and accountability create a healthy community. The work is to design ways to bring citizens (including formal leaders, for they are citizens) together so that they experience the "quality of aliveness" Christopher Alexander writes about. This occurs by being highly attentive to the way that we gather.

- *Strong associational life is essential and central.* Associational life is the volitional aspect of community. It is how citizens choose to build connections for their own sake, usually for common purpose. These are the primary constituency for transformation. In associational life, creating connectedness becomes both an end and a means. Large established systems such as business, government, education, health care, and social services are important but are not essential to community transformation. For systems, building relatedness is mostly a means, not an end in itself.

- **Citizens who use their power to convene other citizens are what create an alternative future.** A quality of aliveness occurs through change efforts that are energized by citizens and are organic or emergent in nature. A shift in the thinking and actions of citizens is more vital than a shift in the thinking and action of institutions and formal leaders. This is in sharp contrast to the traditional beliefs that better leadership, more programs, new funding, new regulations, and more oversight are the path to a better future. At times all of these are necessary, but they do not have the power to create a fundamental shift.

- **The small group is the unit of transformation.** It is in the structure of how small groups gather that an alternative future will be created. This also means that we must set aside our concern for scale and our concern for speed. Scale, speed, and practicality are always the coded arguments for keeping the existing system in place. Belonging can occur through our membership in large groups, but this form of belonging reduces the power of citizens. Instead of surrendering our identity for the sake of belonging, we find in the small group a place that can value our uniqueness.

- **All transformation is linguistic, which means that we can think of community as essentially a conversation.** Then we act on the principle that if we want to change the community, all we have to do is change the conversation. The shift in conversation is from one of problems, fear, and retribution to one of possibility, generosity, and restoration. This is the new context that both creates strong social capital and is created by it.

The overarching intent of these principles is to create communities that operate out of a new context. Transformation can be thought of as a fundamental shift in context, whether the shift is about my own life, my institution, or our community.

Context clearly occurs as individual mindsets, but it also exists as a form of collective worldview. Communities carry a context through the frequently repeated beliefs that citizens hold about the place where they live. The media is one carrier of this context, but it is not its creator.

If transformation is linguistic, then community building requires that we engage in a new conversation, one that we have not had before, one that can create an experience of aliveness and belonging. It is the act of engaging citizens in a new conversation that allows us to act in concert with and actually creates the condition for a new context.

I am using the word *conversation* in a broad sense—namely, all the ways that we listen, speak, and communicate meaning to each other. So, in addition to speaking and listening, this meaning of *conversation* includes the architecture of our buildings and public spaces, the way we inhabit and arrange a room when we come together, and the space we give to the arts.

The Existing Context: Community as a Problem to Be Solved

To make a difference in our community, we must begin by naming the existing context and evolving to a way of thinking that leads to new conversations that produce a new context. It is the shift in conversation that increases social capital. Every time we gather becomes a model of the future we want to create. If you really get this paragraph, you probably don't need to read any further.

Our current context is a long way from one of gifts, generosity, and accountability. The dominant context we now hold is one of deficiencies, interests, and entitlement. Out of this context grows the belief that the suffering of communities is a set of problems to be solved.

After we finish giving speeches about the virtues of our neighborhood and city, we love to elaborate their problems. We have studied and reported for years the problems of housing, health care, the environment, youth at risk, race, the disabled, poverty, unemployment, public education, the crisis in transportation, and drugs. These problems are studied by academics and fueled by talk radio and the AM band, which serves as a place for hosts and citizens to argue, debate, and complain about who is right or wrong and who needs to change. Talk radio and TV are the visible barometers of our attachment to the context giving primacy to problems.

Our love of problems runs deeper than just the joy of complaint, being right, or escape from responsibility. The core belief from which we operate is that an alternative or better future can be accomplished by more problem solving. We believe that defining, analyzing, and studying problems is the way to make a better world. It is the dominant mindset of western culture.

This context—that life is a set of problems to be solved—may actually limit any chance of the future being different from the past. The interest we have in problems is so intense that at some point we take our identity from those problems. Without them, it seems like we would not know who we are as a community. Many of the strongest advocates for change would lose their sense of identity if the change they desired ever occurred.

Community-as-problems-to-be-solved has some benefits. It values the ability to implement, is big on doing, has a certain honesty about it, and worships tangible results as the ultimate blessing. You might say that this is what has gotten us this far. It is not that this (or any other) context is wrong; it just does not have the power to bring something new into the world.

To shift to some other context, we need to detach ourselves from the discussions of problems. One way to achieve this detachment is to see that what we now call problems are simply symptoms of something deeper.

For example, what we call "urban problems" are really symptoms of the breakdown of community. Barry Lopez, well-known author on the environment, lives in a town that several years ago suffered a terrible shooting at its high school. He wrote later that after all the TV cameras, advocates for and against gun control, grief counselors, and experts on youth and public education left town, the citizens could face the reality that the shooting was symptomatic of a breakdown in that community—a breakdown in citizens' capacity to create a place where this kind of tragedy could not happen. His analysis has stayed with me.

The Limitations of Symptoms

The conventional approach to community building and development addresses problem areas such as public safety, jobs and local economy, affordable housing, youth, universal health care, and education. Every city has thousands of institutions, programs, and agencies all committed to serving the public good. From the standpoint of building community and social capital, these institutions and programs are just treating the symptoms. Safety, jobs, housing, and the rest are symptoms of the unreconciled and fragmented nature of the community—what Lopez calls the breakdown of community. This fragmentation or breakdown creates a context where trying to solve the symptoms only sustains them. Otherwise, why have we been working on these symptoms for so long and so hard; and even with so many successful programs, why have we seen too little fundamental change?

The real intent of community transformation is to shift the umbrella under which the traditional problem solving, investment, and social and community action now take place. It is aimed at the restoration of the experience and vitality of community. It is this shift in context, expressed through a shift in language, that creates the conditions where traditional forms of action can create an alternative future.

When we shift from talking about the problems of community to talking about the breakdown of community, something changes. *Naming the challenge as the "breakdown of community" opens the way for restoration.* Holding on to the view that community is a set of problems to be solved holds us in the grip of retribution.

At every level of society, we live in the landscape of retribution. The retributive community is sustained by several aspects of the modern community conversation, which I will expand on throughout the book: the marketing of fear and fault, gravitation toward more laws and oversight, an obsession with romanticized leadership, marginalizing hope and possibility, and devaluing associational life to the point of invisibility.

Getting Our Story About Story Straight

One form of the retributive community conversation is the story we tell ourselves about who we are. Getting clear about the nature of story is important in appreciating the power of the existing context. Especially in those places where history and the past seem overridingly restraining.

Storytelling plays a noble and historic role in our lives and in society. Stories can give us a narrative to guide and instruct us. They are crucial to our knowing who we are; they provide a sense of identity. Some stories, however, become the limitation to creating anything new. Werner Erhard has been so insightful about this. We need to distinguish between the stories that give meaning to our lives and help us find our voice, and those that limit our possibility.

The stories that are useful and fulfilling are the ones that are metaphors, signposts, parables, and inspiration for the fullest expression of our humanity. They are communal teaching stories. Creation stories, wisdom stories, sometimes personal stories that have a mythic quality, even if they come from the person sitting next to me. An example is from Adam Kahane's book on the shifting moment in his work in South Africa, *Solving Tough Problems*. A personal story told for the first time, or shared for the first time in public, can have a transforming effect.

> In Russia, even the past is unpredictable.
>
> Author unknown

Theater, movies, song, literature, and art are storytelling of the highest order. These are the mediums for building an individual sense of what it means to be human. The arts are an essential part of the story of what it means to be a human being and a community.

There are other kinds of stories that in their telling become a limitation. Limiting stories are personal versions of the past. They are stories about the conclusions we drew from events that happened to us. Other limiting stories are those that are rehearsed or make the point that the future will be a slightly modified continuation of the past out of which the story arose. Stories of this nature place us as victims of events or even fate.

Limiting stories are the ones that present themselves as if they were true. Facts. Our stories of our own past are heartfelt and yet are fiction. All we know that is true is that we were born. We may know for sure who our parents, siblings, and other key players in our drama were. But our version of all of them, the meaning and memory that we narrate to all who will listen, is our creation. Made up. Fiction. And this is good news, for it means that a new story can be concocted any time we choose.

Same with community. The stories of violence, crime, wrongdoing that are constantly told are also fiction. The events may have happened, but the versions that let those events define who we are as a community—such as whether it is safe to go downtown, whether we need new leaders, whether people in this place are friendly, whether we are headed up or down—are all fiction. The decision to tell those stories over and over again as if they were defining truths creates the limitation against an alternative future.

This is why therapy and healing is really the process of re-remembering the past in a more forgiving way. The willingness to own up to the fictional nature of our story is where the healing begins. And where the possibility of restoration resides.

In this way, restoration can be considered the willingness to complete and eliminate the power out of the current story we have of our community and our place in it. This creates an opening to produce a new collective story. A new story based on restorative community. One of possibility, generosity, accountability.

CHAPTER 3

The Stuck Community

The existing community context is one that markets fear, assigns fault, and worships self-interest. This context supports the belief that the future will be improved with new laws, more oversight, and stronger leadership. Possibility thinking and associational life are marginalized, relegated to human interest and side stories in the media. The corporate model is the modern ideal, and the economy is the center story. The story in the stuck community defines the role of the media as framer of the debate. In community building, we need to realize that what the media reports is a reflection, not the cause of the conversation that citizens currently hold.

• • •

To create a new story, we first need to come to terms with the current one. This begins by naming it. The story of the stuck community can be heard both in the dominant public debate and also in what we talk to each other about each day. It is important to understand that there is a hidden agenda in every story. This agenda is a point to be made, a political belief about what is important, that stays constant regardless of the events of the day.

Marketing Fear and Fault

The overriding characteristic of the stuck community is the decision to broadcast all the reasons we have to be afraid. This is a kind of advertising that exploits the fear we have of violence, of the urban core, of terrorism, of African-Americans and other ethnic groups, of immigrants, of those who are poor or undereducated, of other religions, and of other countries. It seems like the lead story of every local evening newscast is about crime and human suffering, and if our city had none that day, then we hear how somewhere else in the world someone was murdered, bombed, killed in an accident, or abducted from what was once thought to be a safe place. What we are hearing is the marketing of fear.

In the telling, we are willing to sacrifice the wholeness and dignity of a person for the sake of capturing the emotion or drama of the moment. The marketing of fear thrusts a microphone in the face of someone who has just suffered an irreplaceable loss and asks, "How do you feel?" It is the commercialization of suffering for the sake of profit. Not that complicated.

> When I was deputy press secretary at the White House, our credibility was so bad we couldn't believe our own leaks.
>
> Bill Moyers

The marketing of fear is not just for profit; it also holds a political agenda. Fear justifies the retributive agenda, fundamentalist in the extreme, that has been on the rise for some time. The retributive agenda believes that a just and civil society is one that gives priority to restraints, consequences, and control, and underlines the importance of rules. It gets packaged as spiritual values, family values, the American way, love it or leave it, all under the umbrella of law and order. It helps build the incarceration industry and the protection industry, it creates a platform so that those in power can expand their power, and it discounts the rehabilitation industry. Fear forms the basis of our recent foreign policy and drives much of our legislation. Fear also fuels the allure of suburban life and is a subtle but clear argument against diversity and inclusion.

• • •

In addition to marketing fear, the stuck community markets fault. When there is a human tragedy, most of the energy goes into finding who was to blame. There is a retributive search for responsibility and a corresponding defense from the players claiming their innocence. Fault marketing rests on the belief that if we can assign blame and find cause, it is useful to society and somehow reassures us that it won't happen again. To me, this is irrational thinking. What is missing here is a recognition of the complexity of human affairs, an acknowledgment of the paradoxical and accidental nature of life. There is no insurance policy against the human condition.

Out of the decision to dwell on fear and fault, the community is stuck in a context that holds the following:

- We are a community of problems to be solved. Those who can best articulate the problems and who can best articulate the solutions dominate the conversation.

- The future is defined by the interplay of self-interests, dependent on the accountability of leaders, and controlled by a small number of wealthy and powerful people, commonly lumped into the category we call "they."

- Community action is aimed at eliminating the sources of our fear. We aim at a set of needs and deficiencies. In order to eliminate our fear and respond to the neediness of our people, we try harder at what we have been doing all along. We lock down neighborhoods, build more prisons, and reduce tolerance to zero. We call for better programs, more expertise, more funding, better leadership, stronger consequences, and more protection. We are committed to trying harder at what is not working.

Ramping Up Laws and Oversight

When something goes wrong, we carry the illusion that after we find the guilty party, some kind of legislation or change in policy will prevent the crime or accident from happening again. We are stuck in the belief that we can legislate the future and mandate morality. In Cincinnati we passed an ordinance that street people had to be licensed to ask passersby for money. The idea was that somehow I now would be comfortable going downtown knowing that the person asking for money had been certified and approved by the city council. Now even panhandling was professionalized. The ordinance did not bring more people into town at night.

The concern about street safety and increasing the comfort and quality of the urban experience is of course legitimate. What limits us and undermines our quest for authentic community is the belief that fault finding, legislation, and enforcement can give us the security we seek. But this thinking is just too simplistic and reductionist. It is more a response to our need to take action and look like problem solvers, rather than finding a durable answer to a complex civic issue.

A corollary to more laws is the push for more oversight. We think that more watching improves performance. All the evidence is to the contrary, for most high-performing communities and organizations are heavily self-regulating. My favorite quote on this is "Research causes cancer in rats." It is reasonable to understand that the act of oversight may in fact increase the very thing that is being watched with the intent of reducing it.

The political agenda of the stuck community says that citizens and employees are incapable of monitoring themselves and controlling each other, and that more careful oversight, institutionally mandated and installed, will build community and provide for the common good. It is in fact an argument against building community and ends up leaving us more dependent on specialists and special designees of the state. It provides the argument for monarchy. Someone to watch over me.

Romanticizing Leadership

Carole Schurch was taking care of the logistics of a conference on transformation. She opened the event by announcing, "The restrooms are down the hall on the left, lunch will be at 1:00 p.m., dinner is at 8:00 p.m., and the conference will be over tomorrow afternoon. Let me know if I can help you with anything and also let me know what time your mother is picking you up!"

We love our habit of dependency and accept the culture of retribution because it reinforces the case for strong leaders—"strong" being the code word for autocratic, a message our culture is increasingly willing to accede to. We are fascinated with our leaders. We speak endlessly, both in the public conversation and privately, about the rise and fall of leaders. The agenda this sustains is that leaders are cause and all others are effect. That all that counts is what leaders do. That leaders are the leverage point for building a better community. That they are foreground while citizens, followers, players, and anyone else not in a leadership position is background. This is a deeply patriarchal agenda, and it is this love of leaders that limits our capacity to create an alternative future. It proposes that the only real accountability in the world is at the top. They are the only ones worth talking about.

The effect of buying in to this view of leadership is that it lets citizens off the hook and breeds citizen dependency and entitlement. It undermines a culture where each is accountable for their community. The attention on the leader makes good copy, it gives us someone to blame and thereby declares our innocence, but it does not contribute to building community. In its own way, it reinforces individualism, putting us in the stance of waiting for the cream to rise, wishing for a great individual to bring light where there was darkness.

What is missing or dismissed here are the community-building insights about how groups work, the power of relatedness, what occurs when ordinary people get together. We write communal possibility off as just another meeting, the blind leading the blind, citizens coming together to pool ignorance or to speak "truth to power," which is just a complaint session in evening clothes.

As an aside, to return to in more depth later, some reasons for discounting the power of citizens are well founded, for most of the time when citizens come together it makes no difference. That's because they operate under the retributive principles that I am trying to describe in this section. They want to define the problem, find fault, elaborate fear, demand control-oriented action, and point to leaders. Many citizens get engaged in community only when they are angry.

If we keep engaging citizens in this traditional way, then no amount of involvement will make a difference. The way we currently gather has no transformational power. This is what needs to change, for if we do not change the way citizens come together, if we do not shift the context under which we gather and do not change the methodology of our gatherings, then we will have to keep waiting for great leaders, and we will never step up to the power and accountability that is within our grasp.

Marginalizing Possibility

Given the dominant context that values scarcity, leadership, individualism, fear, and fault, anything positive or hopeful becomes an anomaly. An exception, an accident. To choose possibility means I have to confront cynicism. Journalism, human services, corrections, and public safety are professions that claim their cynicism comes from constant contact and familiarity with the dark side of society. This ignores the reality that what you see comes from what you choose to look at. Decide that all the news fit to print is about problems, and that is what you get. In the retributive culture, cynicism is the norm and becomes the lead story. Cynicism justifies retribution. Retribution is fueled by cynicism.

In this context, possibility and vision become buried in the middle section of the news, or become an upbeat pat on the back as the anchor goes off the air. Possibility and faith are seen as threatening because they are an indictment of cynicism. So it is not by accident that when citizens do find a way to use their gifts, or commit to something thought impossible, or bring faith and gratitude into the world, the story is reduced to a "human interest" piece—the kiss of death when it comes to changing our context. Many reporters do not even consider these stories journalism.

This is one way possibility is trivialized. When labeled "human interest," possibility doesn't qualify as news. It is a feel-good diversion. Something to calm our nerves. Possibility and the faith that supports it may be strong declarations for the individual, but for the collective, they are neutered and treated as merely charming.

Possibility also gets undermined by being confused with optimism. Even when leaders speak to the possibility of our community, in the stuck community we consider it a motivational speech, a sales pitch, a bootstrap keynote to make people feel better, to lift our spirits from what we call reality. But possibility is not a prediction, or a goal; it is a choice to bring a certain quality into our lives. Optimism, which *is* a prediction about the future, has no power. Pessimism is equally irrelevant.

The ways in which possibility is marginalized underline the importance of context. All that does not confirm the prevailing mindset is made marginal and cute. This is why, if you want to create an alternative future, you have to shift the context, for all that disconfirms the current context will be discarded. We need to shift what is considered "reality." For example, if we see the media as a reflection of who we are, why not value with our listening the media that promotes learning and possibility, documents miracles, and reports on a different agenda, and call it the "new reality"? Les Ihara, a longtime state senator in Hawaii, says that what is needed is "a shift in the ground of being that reports the news." If we take that seriously, as factual and true, then something new is brought into the world.

Devaluing Associational Life

John McKnight has studied communities for 30 years and found that community is built most powerfully by what he calls "associational life," referring to the myriad ways citizens come together to do good work and serve the public interest. Whether in clubs, associations, informal gatherings, special events, or just on the street or at breakfast, neighborly contact constitutes an uncounted and unnoticed glue and connection that makes good communities work.

The stuck community essentially discounts associational life and instead values, and even glorifies, the "system" life, especially the private sector and corporate mindset. This context is so around us that we have become anaesthetized to it. Although there is a growing awareness of the cost of this mindset (see David Korten), we still act as if what is good for business is good for the country.

Here are some ways in which we discount associational life, the place where the social fabric is built:

- **The only true measure of community is its economic prosperity.** We seek the American dream, streets paved with gold. The only good news that makes the news is when Toyota decides to build a plant in our town. Communities will justify spending infinite amounts of money to keep sports teams because they are theoretically good for the economy. Job creation is the final argument for most of our mistakes.

- We name social service and institutions that serve the public good "not for profits." "Not for profit" means that service and generosity are defined by what it is not. What kind of identity and esteem does this establish for the choice for service and care for community? Can you imagine introducing yourself as the name you are *not?* "Hello, my name is not Alice." "Well, I would like you to meet my friend, not Roger." There is no identity in that. Nothing memorable or recognizable next time we meet. There is a movement to call it the "public benefit" sector. Not such a bad thing.

- Associations are under constant pressure to be more corporate: to merge, become more efficient, submit to external oversight, measure harder, and submit to greater accountability. These are core values in the private sector. A natural outgrowth of this is the way many foundations, which exist for the sake of community service, treat corporations as their clients. In the philanthropic world you also hear people talk about their "return on social investment." We use the language of commerce when talking about the field of generosity.

- The public benefit sector makes front page news only when there is scandal. The head of a large agency who spends funds on limousines and high living is front page for days. When the same agency softens the landing for people in a tragedy or turns people's lives around, the story is at best a footnote.

- We marginalize compassion in the public conversation. Here's an example: As an effort to build the image and well-being of the city, Go Cincinnati is about streetcars, housing development, and attracting new businesses. It sells hard the strengths of the city, including the arts, entertainment, and sports attractions. All good things to sell and essential to a city that works. What is missing in this conversation and sales pitch is the compassion of a city. Having a large number of social services in a neighborhood is seen as a weakness, not a selling point. The view is that if people need help, if they are vulnerable or in crisis, it is a communal liability. The generosity that serves these people goes unmentioned as an asset.

Reinforcing Self-Interest and Isolation

These dimensions of the way we talk about our community and the dominant stories we tell about our community work together to create an insular mentality. Under the siege of fear, fault, and the rest, people and institutions build a wall around themselves and are primarily concerned with their own survival. This gives us a community where each sector—business, education, government, social service, health care—is so focused on its own affairs that those who choose to commit to the well-being of the whole have a difficult time gaining a foothold.

And what exists for our institutions is reinforced by citizens. Citizens mostly get engaged when something threatens their backyard. They show up in public settings when they are angry; they become activated by narrowly defined interests.

Both institutions and active citizens are sincere and often effective in the pursuit of their own well-being, of matters that occur within their own boundaries. But no matter how effective they are in pursuing their interests, the community as a whole does not change, especially for those on the margin. In an individualistic culture, the social capital, the fabric of community, does not get built.

To summarize, the context of retribution and the story that grows out of it cause our attempts to build community to be what actually keeps it unchanged. Our retributive approach to the symptoms of poverty, violence, homelessness, and cynicism does not create these symptoms but interferes with their changing. Retribution by its nature serves to fragment community and reduce social capital. The side effect is that each citizen's accountability for the well-being of community is reduced. When the context is retributive, reduced accountability and diminished social capital are the direct outgrowths of our very efforts to improve community. And this mostly occurs as an unintended consequence, for no one holds a fragmented community as a goal.

The retributive context, given form through the dominant public conversation, is based on a culture of fear, fault finding, fragmentation, and worrying more about taxes than compassion; it is more about being right than working something out, more about gerrymandering for our own interests than giving voice to those on the margin. Other than that, it is fine.

The Media

As a key messenger of context in the stuck community, the media takes its cue from citizens and makes its living from retribution. The public conversation most visible to us is the interaction between what we citizens want to hear and the narrative put forth by the media. But it is too easy to blame the media for valuing entertainment over news and for selling fear and problems over generosity and possibility. It is more useful to see that the media is a reflection of who we, as citizens, have become.

The news is most usefully understood as the daily decisions about what is newsworthy. This is a power that goes way beyond simply informing us. The agenda in each story defines what is important, and in doing this, it promotes an identity for a community.

> The problem, of course, was that Baba saw the world in black and white. And he got to decide what was black and white.
>
> Khaled Hosseini,
> *The Kite Runner*

This means the real importance of the media is not in the typical debate over the quality, balance, or even accuracy of what is reported. These vary with the channel, the network, the newspaper, the Web site. They vary with having the resources to get the whole story, the market segment it is aiming at, and its editorial agenda. What is most important, and the power that is most defining, is the power of the media to decide what is worth talking about. As British newspaper pioneer Lord Northcliffe once said, "News is what somebody somewhere wants to suppress; all the rest is advertising."

The media's power is the power to name the public debate. Or, in other words, the power to name "reality." This is true for the mainstream as well as online media.

The point is this: Citizens have the capacity to change the community story, to reclaim the power to name what is worth talking about, to bring a new context into being. Those of us who create the current dominant context for the community conversation drive the conditions that nurture a retributive context or a retributive community. If we do not choose to change this context and the strategies that follow from it, we will produce no new outcomes for our institutions, neighborhoods, and towns.

CHAPTER 4

The Restorative Community

Restoration comes *from the choice to value possibility and relatedness over problems, self-interest, and the rest of the stuck community's agenda. It hinges on the accountability chosen by citizens and their willingness to connect with each other around promises they make to each other.*

Restoration is created by the kinds of conversations we initiate with each other. These conversations are the leverage point for an alternative future. The core question that underlies each conversation is "What can we create together?" Shifting the context from retribution to restoration will occur through language that moves in the following directions: from problems to possibility; from fear and fault to gifts, generosity, and abundance; from law and oversight to social fabric and chosen accountability; from corporation and systems to associational life; and from leaders to citizens.

• • •

In contrast to the isolating effects of retribution, a restorative experience, relationship, or community produces new energy rather than holding us in place. Restoration is associated with the quality of aliveness and wholeness that Christopher Alexander talks about. This quality is not only in the artifacts, buildings, and spaces that he refers to, but also in the gatherings and conversations we choose to create. The energy crisis we face is not so much about fossil fuels as it is about the calcified experience that is too often created by the way we hold conversations, both publicly and when we come together in more private settings.

Restorative community is created when we allow ourselves to use the language of healing and relatedness and belonging without embarrassment. It recognizes that taking responsibility for one's own part in creating the present situation is the critical act of courage and engagement, which is the axis around which the future rotates. The essence of restorative community building is not economic prosperity or the political discourse or the capacity of leadership; it is citizens' willingness to own up to their contribution, to be humble, to choose accountability, and to have faith in their own capacity to make authentic promises to create the alternative future.

This means that the essential aspect of the restoration of community is a context in which each citizen chooses to be accountable rather than entitled.

Accountability is the willingness to care for the whole, and it flows out of the kind of conversations we have about the new story we want to take our identity from. It means we have conversations of what we can do to create the future. Entitlement is a conversation about what others can or need to do to create the future for us.

Restoration begins when we think of community as a possibility, a declaration of the future that we choose to live into. This idea of a communal possibility is distinct from what we commonly call an individual possibility. Community is something more than a collection of individual longings, desires, or possibilities. The communal possibility has its own landscape, and its own dynamics, requirements, and points of leverage. In the individualistic world we live in, we can congregate a large collection of self-actualized people and still not hold the idea or experience of community.

The communal possibility rotates on the question "What can we create together?" This emerges from the social space we create when we are together. It is shaped by the nature of the culture within which we operate but is not controlled by it. This question of what we can create together is at the intersection of possibility and accountability. Possibility without accountability results in a wishful thinking. Accountability without possibility creates despair, for even if we know we are creating the world we exist in, we cannot imagine its being any different from the past that got us here.

Example: The Clermont Counseling Center

Tricia Burke is the director of the Clermont Counseling Center. She completely understands the destructive power of labeling and categorizing human beings. Rare for one in a leadership position in a labeling industry. One of her programs is for women in abusive relationships who are survivors of domestic violence. She calls this program Women of Worth. What's in a name . . . everything.

The counseling center also runs a mental health facility, and this is the story I want to pay attention to. It contains most of the elements of freedom, choice, transforming language, and small group belonging discussed in this book. In the mental health program are clients who are labeled as paranoid schizophrenic, bipolar, and delusional, and have a history of state hospital stays. For the center to bill Medicaid for their services, the services must be "medically necessary." This means they are required to certify each client's illness and medicalize all of the center's services in order to be reimbursed.

In the eyes of Tricia and her staff, many of the most effective healing efforts come from actions that are not really medical interventions. What are often most healing are the ways that people in programs like the center's discover to have fun, embraced and surrounded by the support of others like themselves. The sense of belonging that accrues is as healing as traditional treatment. This sort of thing is not a legitimate program activity in the eyes of Medicaid. To keep Medicaid funding, the center is required to name and place a disease on the head of each person.

Despite this, Tricia and her staff decided to change the conversation at Clermont in dramatic ways. They gave up the Medicaid funding for their "partial hospital day treatment" program and put the clients in charge of the day program. Staff were reassigned to other programs. In doing this, Tricia changed the message to clients from one focusing on their liabilities to one focusing on their possibilities. The organizing questions to "members"—no longer patients—were "What do you like to do?" and "How do you want to fill your day?" While the traditional hospital experiences were maintained, these questions were the organizing principles that guided the healing process.

The strategy then was to treat members as if they had the capacity to design and structure a good portion of their own time. Phoenix Place, the new name chosen by the clients for this effort, became a controlled self-governing program. There was only one paid staff member—Kim Hensley, the director of the program—and many of the governance and program decisions were placed in the hands of members.

In the first year, the members came up with ingenious answers to the question "What can we create together?" For example:

- They formed and chose an executive committee for themselves.
- They organized a wellness activity.
- They volunteered their services to an animal shelter.
- They wanted to travel, so they decided to open a snack shop to earn money.
- When Phoenix Place received a grant to do medication education for other mentally ill folk in five counties, the members did this education.
- When Ohio state legislators were invited to visit the facility, the members wanted time with them to make the point that people who have mental illness are not their illness, they are much more than their illness.
- They were no longer afraid to talk about their lives; they came out of the closet.
- The group started training police on the nature of mental illness—what it is like to hear voices, for example. They taught the police how to approach people having an incident and what language to use.
- They started a journaling process, which they called WildSpirits, to give voice to what it feels like to be in the dark hole of despair and find your way out, and to express their healing by writing about hope, gratitude, love . . .

At the end of the first year of Phoenix Place, its members felt pride in what they had created; they had jobs to do and had regained some of the roles they had lost in the larger society. Most of all, they had begun to once again have hopes and dreams about their future.

Eventually they outgrew the small house for Phoenix Place, so they set about raising money for a bigger one by working the concession stands at the Reds and Bengals games—and years later their dream came true. When it did, they wrote a grant to make a video to tell their story.

Of course the story of Phoenix Place, and others like it, is not all about success and victory. Along the way, Tricia says, it took patience and encouragement to help Phoenix members shift their thinking to believing that they could run their own program. In the beginning, they were angry and felt they were being abandoned. They even picketed the center. Helping them break free of their dependency was difficult.

Here is a part I especially like: One exercise was for individuals to complete a questionnaire about their strengths as part of a program on positive psychology. The members noted that this was the first time in their lives they had ever taken a test and gotten good news from the results.

The transition from patient to citizen is always difficult. For all of us, not just labeled people. And the trajectory is not always smooth. When the original director of Phoenix Place left, it caused anxiety and worry. The member-led executive committee began to act superior, controlling, and judgmental, and some of the spirit of community waned. In other words, they started to function like most traditional executive committees.

The group rediscovered their balance when a new director was selected, and the members mostly became friends once again. But their temporary fall from grace shows that we can never forget how fragile is our ability to hold our freedom and stay whole in hard times.

Lessons from Restorative Justice

Phoenix Place gives us a powerful model of what a restorative community looks like. When I say "restorative," I am not talking about returning to a prior time, fixing up an old building, or seeking to recapture a culture that we think once existed. Restoration is about healing our woundedness—in community terms, healing our fragmentation and incivility. It is only out of this healing that something new can emerge.

I have been attracted for some time by the way *restorative* is used in the criminal justice system, which I learned from Barry Stuart and others who have created the restorative justice movement. They have given a powerful structure to restoration, and they have done it in a most unlikely place. The intent of restoration in the criminal justice system is to provide a more healing path for both the offender and victim of a crime. This becomes an option for the victim to choose and for the offender to agree to. It also gives a voice to the community, for the community is also wounded by a crime.

There are several steps to restoration: The offender admits to the crime, the offender and the victim and their families talk of the cost and damage the crime has caused to all their lives, the offender apologizes for the offense, the offender promises not to do it again, and the offender agrees to some form of restitution for the damage caused.

Finally, the victim and their family decide whether to forgive the offender and accept the restitution. If they decide to forgive, then the representatives of the community have a voice in deciding whether to allow the offender to go free and rejoin the community. If the victim and their family decide not to forgive, then the offender goes through the regular criminal justice process. On a global scale, restorative justice is similar to the practices of the Truth and Reconciliation Commission in South Africa.

These steps contain many of the elements of community building. It is not so much the methodology that concerns us here, but rather the context and spirit that these movements offer us. They show that an alternative to retribution is possible and has worked in the world. This spirit of restoration promises a different future for our communities.

Community as Conversation

The idea of community restoration becomes concrete when we grasp the importance of language. When we understand that, we can see how our language, or conversation, is the action step that makes creating an alternative future possible. Suppose we begin to think of our communities as nothing more or less than a conversation.

Every community has its buildings, leaders, schools, landscape, but for the moment let us say that these are not what make a community unique or define its identity. Instead it is useful to declare that the aspect of a community that gives it a new possibility is simply the conversation it chooses to have with itself. Jane Jacobs, world expert on neighborhoods, understands this. When she was asked why she thought Portland, Oregon, has been so successful in creating a habitable community, she said the only thing unique about Portland is that "Portlanders love Portland." In our terms here, it was the conversation Portlanders had with each other about their town that made the difference.

Thus if we speak of change or transformation in our city or town—in my case, Cincinnati—we are referring to the conversation that is occurring in that town. We do this not because it is the whole picture, but because it is the part of the picture that is most amenable to change.

This means the alternative future we speak of takes form when we realize that the only powerful place from which to take our identity may be the conversation that we are. We begin the process of restoration when we understand that our well-being is defined simply by the nature and structure and power of our conversation.

The future of a community then becomes a choice between a retributive conversation (a problem to be solved) and a restorative conversation (a possibility to be lived into). Restoration is a possibility brought into being by choosing that kind of conversation. And with that conversation it becomes real and tangible, for once we have declared a possibility, and done so with a sense of belonging and in the presence of others, that possibility has been brought into the room, and thus into the institution, into the community.

The key phrase here is "in the presence of others." A possibility, when declared publicly, heard and witnessed by others with whom we have a common interest, at a moment when something is at stake, is a critical element of communal transformation. This public conversation creates a larger relatedness and transcends a simply individual transformation. Conversations of possibility gone public are not all that restores, but without them, personal and private conversations of possibility have no political currency and therefore no communal power.

The Shift

To summarize the story line to this point, our conversations and gatherings have the power to shift the context from retributive community to restorative community. This occurs through questions and dialogue that move us in the following directions:

- From conversations about problems to ones of possibility
- From conversations about fear and fault to ones of gifts, generosity, and abundance
- From a bet on law and oversight to a preference for building the social fabric and choosing accountability
- From seeing the corporation and systems as central to seeing associational life as central
- From a focus on leaders to a focus on citizens

What these have in common is the movement from centrism and individualism to pluralism and interdependent communalism. This shift has important consequences for our communities. It offers to return politics to public service and restore our trust in leadership. It moves us from having faith in professionals and those in positions of authority to having faith in our neighbors. It takes us into a context of hospitality, wherein we welcome strangers rather than believing we need to protect ourselves from them. It changes our mindset from valuing what is efficient to valuing the importance of belonging. It helps us to leave behind our penchant for seeing our disconnectedness as an inevitable consequence of modern life and moves us toward accountability and citizenship.

CHAPTER 5

Taking Back Our Projections

Citizens become powerful when they choose to shift the context within which they act in the world. Using the language of context rather than culture puts the choice into our own hands. It acknowledges that our mindset, even our worldview, is subjective and therefore amenable to change.

To choose a context conducive to citizenship, we first need to understand the idea of communal projection. Projection is the act of attributing qualities to others that we deny within ourselves. It is expressed in the way we label others and then build diagnostic categories and whole professions around the labeling. The shift away from projection and labeling provides the basis for defining what we mean by authentic citizenship—which is to hold ourselves accountable for the well-being of the larger community and to choose to own and exercise power rather than defer or delegate it to others.

• • •

Here is a way of thinking about the shift in context from retribution to restoration. We begin with going deeper into what it means to choose to be accountable, not just for ourselves but for the world. The reason the retributive context cannot improve the conditions it tries to heal is that it talks a lot about accountability but does not embody it. The context of retribution itself is actually an ongoing argument against accountability. The marketing of fear and fault and the love of leadership have in common the belief that something or someone else is the problem and that the someone else needs to do something different before anything can profoundly get better.

To inquire more deeply into this shift in context, we need to focus on the distinction between culture and context. The common thinking holds that transformation requires a culture change. I am talking here about context, not culture. The reason I use the word *context* versus *culture* is to construct our stance as a matter of choice. Culture is a set of shared values that emerges from the history of experience and the story that is produced out of that. It is the past that gives us our identity and corrals our behavior in order to preserve that identity. Context is the way we see the world. See the world, not remember the world.

We conventionally think that our view of the world is based on history, events, evidence, and this pattern is treated as fact and is decisive. It is called fact but is only a collective memory, which in the glare of the midday sun I would irreverently call fiction. If this thing we call context were fact, then it would not be amenable to transformation.

If context were inevitable and purely based on fact, then we would be condemned to live in fear. We are constantly being sold the fear curriculum so that, in time, we begin to think the context of fear is for good cause and data based. In reality, fear rises and falls for more reasons than events would dictate. If you can entertain the thought that fear is the curriculum of the patriarchal element of our culture, then we can understand that the dominant fear conversation is as much a result of marketing and product promotion as it is a response to facts. In the domain of public safety, for instance, there is little relationship between the crime rate and people's attitude about danger. There is evidence that many kinds of crime went down in many major cities in the late '90s and early 2000s. But while crime went down, the public's fear of crime went up. Why? Because while crime was going down, the reporting of crime went up. So the determinant of our fear is partly the retributive agenda, which leads to reporting about how dangerous the world is, and, more important, our choice to buy the story.

Here is the point: In the retributive context, fear, fault, dependency on leaders, cynicism, and indifference to associational life act as if they are evidence based. If we are committed to a future distinct from the past, then we treat them as a matter of choice, and we call this context, not culture.

Projection and Labeling

If the fear-retribution cycle is a matter of choice and not an inevitable result of culture, then we have to face the fact that the choice to inhale it must mean it offers us payoffs.

One payoff for believing that problems and the suffering in our cities are the inevitable products of modern life and culture is that it lets us off the hook. The payoff begins the moment we believe that problems reside in others and that they are the ones who need to change. We displace or assign to others certain qualities that have more to do with us than with them. This is called *projection*, an idea most of us are quite familiar with. I discuss it here because if we do not take back our projection, a new context and conversation are simply not possible. The essence of our projection is that it places accountability for an alternative future on others. This is the payoff of stereotyping, prejudice, and a bunch of "isms" that we are all familiar with. This is what produces the "other." The reward is that it takes the pressure off of us. It is a welcome escape from our freedom. We project onto leaders the qualities or disappointments that we find too much to carry ourselves. We project onto the stranger, the wounded, the enemy those aspects of ourselves that are too much to own.

Projection denies the fact that my view of the "other" is my creation, and this is especially true with how we view our communities and the people in them. Most simply, how I view the other is an extension or template of how I view myself. This insight is the essence of being accountable. To be accountable is to act as an owner and creator of what exists in the world, including the light and dark corners of my own existence. It is the willingness to focus on what we can do in the face of whatever the world presents to us. Accountability does not project or deny; accountability is the willingness to see the whole picture that resides within, even what is not so pretty.

We are generally familiar with these ideas from the psychology of projection for individuals, and the point here is that projection also works more broadly at the level of profession, institution, and community.

Take poverty, for example. When we see low-income people, we focus on their needs and deficiencies, and that is all we see. We think their poverty is central to who they are, and that is all they are. We believe that the poor have created that condition for themselves. We view them with charity or pity and wring our hands at their plight. At this moment we are projecting our own vulnerability onto the poor. It is a defense against not only my own vulnerability, but also my complicity in creating poverty.

If we took back this projection, we would stop denying that each of us plays a role in creating poverty—by our way of living, by our indifference, by our labeling them "poor" as if that is who they are, by our choice not to have them as neighbors and get to know them. Part of the reduce-taxes debate is the belief that we are wasting money on "those people." It is not that the people we project onto do not have some of the qualities we see; it is that the meaning we give to what we see—in this case, the label and categorization—is just projection. It's the same with the unemployed, with broken homes, neighborhoods, youth on the street, and all the other symptoms we live with.

> "You pushed my buttons."
> "I know, but I didn't install them."
> Author unknown

The projection is the attribution we make, the conclusions we draw, and the fact that all we see in them is what is missing. When we believe that the "other" is the problem and that transformation is required of them and not of us, we become the beneficiaries of their suffering in the world. Some of us make a living off of their deficiencies. We study their needs, devise professions to service them, create institutions dependent on the existence of these deficiencies. All done with sincere intent and in the name of virtue.

In our philanthropy, this mindset that the "other" is the problem means that we need to wait for them to change before the change we want in the world can come to pass. And until they change, we need to stay distant and contain them. This diverts us from the realization that we have the means, the tools, the thinking to create a world we want to inhabit, and to do it for all. If we saw others as another aspect of ourselves, we would welcome them into our midst. We would let them know that they belong, that they are neighbors, with all their complexity.

• • •

To continue, as a community, to focus on the needs and deficiencies of the most vulnerable is not an act of hospitality. It substitutes labeling for welcoming. It is isolating in that they become a special category of people, defined by what they cannot do. This isolates the most vulnerable. Despite our care for them, we do not welcome them into our midst, we service them. They become objects. This may be why it is easier to raise money for suffering in distant places or to celebrate the history of slavery's end than it is to raise money for our neighbors on the margin who are six blocks away. Their proximity stands in the way of our compassion. Example: In Cincinnati we have spent $110 million to construct a magnificent Freedom Center to celebrate the end of slavery. Six blocks away we have citizens living in very difficult conditions—and there is great reluctance to see the relationship between the two. We are willing to acclaim the victories of the past; and yet, caught in our projection onto the poor, we sustain a rather negative attitude toward the suffering of people down the street.

To be even more specific about projection, it shows up in communities through the conversations that focus on any of the needs, problems, and diagnostic categories through which we label others. For example, we limit our future when we frame conversations in the following ways:

- Young people on the corner or out of school become "youth at risk."

- People who served their time in jail become "ex-offenders."

- People who live on the street become "homeless" or "vagrants."

- Those with physical or mental challenges become "handicapped" and "bipolar."

- Immigrants become "illegals."

And the list goes on based on the mood of the times.

This labeling, and the services that flow out of it, is the "commercialization of needs" that John McKnight has written about. It becomes the justification for the fear and fault conversation that in turn justifies the context of retribution. Which in turn drives all the programs, expertise, and policy that we thought were going to make the difference. When the projection is reclaimed and the labels abandoned, the justification disappears and space is created for a welcoming, gift-oriented restoration.

Taking Back the Projection

Restoration and reconciliation begin the moment we take back our projection and reduce the labeling in the name of service. This is a key to transformation. The moment we choose to change this conversation, the moment we choose to end the projection-and-labeling cycle, transformation happens.

One thing seems certain: When we stay isolated, there is no way to take back the communal projection. No amount of inner work or healing as individuals will be powerful. Projection sustains itself in the absence of relatedness, in places where we have no sense of belonging. It cannot be taken back by acting alone. It does not disappear no matter how much data is presented, no matter how much moral suasion or guilt we try to produce. "Why can't we all just get along?" was a poignant plea, but it had no power to join us together.

Communal transformation, taking back our collective projections, occurs when people get connected to those who were previously strangers, and when we invite people into conversations that ask them to act as creators or owners of community. It occurs when we become related in a new way to those we are intending to help. This means we stop labeling others for their deficiencies and focus on their gifts.

Example: Elementz

One example where youth are valued rather than labeled is a center in Cincinnati named Elementz. A group of young people have created a hip-hop center where 14- to 24-year-olds can spend three nights a week learning about writing, performing, disc jockeying, and producing hip-hop music. Their music. They also learn about graffiti as an art form and break dancing as a form of entertainment. Elementz takes the very things that bother many adults—the music, the dancing, the graffiti—and treats them as gifts. This is not a recreation center; it is a learning space where youth have to attend programs in order to be in the building.

Elementz was conceived by young people and young people run it, so that when youth from the street walk into the building, they see a reflection of themselves and know they are welcome. The staff of the place are not professionally trained "youth workers," they are young people two steps further down the road who have made a commitment and sacrifice to care for those coming behind them.

The goal of Elementz is not specifically to provide careers in these entertainment fields—that would be making a promise that is unreal. The goal is to give to youth an experience of what they can create, a sense of the value they have inside of them. The ultimate goal is to offer them a new possibility for their lives.

Nothing guarantees that a young person will see a new possibility, but we can create the conditions where that choice is more likely. The transformation we seek occurs when these two conditions are created: when we produce deeper relatedness across boundaries, and when we create new conversations that focus on the gifts and capacities of others.

This allows us to focus on our connectedness rather than on our differences. We no longer need to take our identity from being right about "them" or from continuing to see "them" as individuals with needs or as people somehow less than us. It puts an end to our need to declare victory. The differences, instead of being problems to solve, become a source of vitality, a gift. In the language of community transformation, this is what it means to be accountable. At these moments, we become owners, with the free will capable of creating the world we want to inhabit. We become citizens.

CHAPTER 6

What It Means to Be a Citizen

Choosing to be accountable for the whole, creating a context of hospitality and collective possibility, acting to bring the gifts of those on the margin into the center—these are some of the ways we begin to create a community of citizens. To reclaim our citizenship is to be accountable, and this comes from the inversion of what is cause and what is effect. When we are open to thinking along the lines that citizens create leaders, that children create parents, and that the audience creates the performance, we create the conditions for widespread accountability and the commitment that emerges from it. This inversion may not be the whole truth, but it is useful.

• • •

If what holds the possibility of an alternative future for our community is our capacity to fully come into being as a citizen, then we have to talk about this word *citizen*. Our definition here is that a citizen is one who is willing to be accountable for and committed to the well-being of the whole. That whole can be a city block, a community, a nation, the earth. A citizen is one who produces the future, someone who does not wait, beg, or dream for the future.

The antithesis of being a citizen is the choice to be a consumer or a client, an idea that John McKnight again has been so instructive about. Consumers give power away. They believe that their own needs can be best satisfied by the actions of others—whether those others are elected officials, top management, social service providers, or the shopping mall. Consumers also allow others to define their needs. If leaders and service providers are guilty of labeling or projecting onto others the "needs" to justify their own style of leadership or service that they provide, consumers collude with them by accepting others' definition of their needs. This provider-consumer transaction is the breeding ground for entitlement, and it is unfriendly to our definition of citizen and the power inherent in that definition.

The Meaning of Citizenship

The conventional definition of citizenship is concerned with the act of voting and taking a vow to uphold the constitution and laws of a country. This is narrow and limiting. Too many organizations that are committed to sustaining democracy in the world and at home have this constrained view of citizenship. Citizenship is not about voting, or even about having a vote. To construe the essence of citizenship primarily as the right to vote reduces its power—as if voting ensures a democracy. It is certainly a feature of democracy, but as Fareed Zakaria points out in his book *The Future of Freedom,* the right to vote does not guarantee a civil society, or in our terms a restorative one.

When we think of citizens as just voters, we reduce them to being consumers of elected officials and leaders. We see this most vividly at election time, when candidates become products, issues become the message, and the campaign is a marketing and distribution system for the selling of the candidate. Great campaign managers are great marketers and product managers. Voters become target markets, demographics, whose most important role is to meet in focus groups to respond to the nuances of message. This is the power of the consumer, which is no power at all.

Through this lens, we can understand why so many people do not vote. They do not believe their action can impact the future. It is partly a self-chosen stance and partly an expression of the helplessness that grows out of a retributive world. This way of thinking is not an excuse not to vote, but it does say that our work is to build the capacity of citizens to be accountable and to become creators of community.

• • •

We can see most clearly how we marginalize the real meaning of *citizen* when the word becomes politicized as part of the retributive debate. We argue over undocumented workers, immigration, and the rights of ex-felons—and even their children. We politicize the issue of English as the official language and building a new wall on the Rio Grande that we will have to tear down someday.

Citizenship as the willingness to build community gets displaced by isolationism in any form. It is not by accident that the loudest activists for finding and deporting undocumented workers are some of the leaders of the fear, oversight, safety, and security agenda. They are the key beneficiaries of the retributive society. If we want community, we have to be unwilling to allow citizenship to be co-opted in this way.

The idea of what it means to be a citizen is too important and needs to be taken back to its more profound value. Citizenship is a state of being. It is a choice for activism and care. A citizen is one who is willing to do the following:

- Hold oneself accountable for the well-being of the larger collective of which we are a part.

- Choose to own and exercise power rather than defer or delegate it to others.

- Enter into a collective possibility that gives hospitable and restorative community its own sense of being.

- Acknowledge that community grows out of the possibility of citizens. Community is built not by specialized expertise, or great leadership, or improved services; it is built by great citizens.

- Attend to the gifts and capacities of all others, and act to bring the gifts of those on the margin into the center.

The Inversion of Cause

To create communities where citizens reclaim their power, we need to shift our beliefs about who is in charge and where power resides. We need to invert our thinking about what is cause and what is effect. This is what has the capacity to confront our entitlement and dependency.

Being powerful means that my experience, my discovery, even my pleasure are mine to create. This view has us see how audiences create performances, children create parents, students create teachers, and citizens create leaders.

It is not that this shift of cause is necessarily true, but it gives us power. In every case it puts choice into our own hands instead of having us wait for the transformation of others to give us the future we desire. If our intention is to create the possibility of an alternative future, then we need a future formed by our own hands. A handcrafted future.

> The chicken is the egg's way of reproducing itself.
>
> Peter Koestenbaum

Inverting our thinking does not change the world, but it creates a condition where the shift in the world becomes possible. The shift is the inversion in our thinking. The step from thinking of ourselves as effect to thinking of ourselves as cause is the act of inversion that creates a culture of citizen accountability. This is the point upon which accountability revolves.

A note: The cause-and-effect, Cartesian clockwork view of the world not only overstated the mechanical nature of the world, but it also put cause at the wrong end of the equation. Double indemnity.

This inversion challenges conventional wisdom that believes there is one right way. And by "inversion" I mean a real inversion: 180 degrees, not 179 degrees. This is not time for compromise or balance. Inverting our thinking about cause and effect gives support to really challenge "the way things work." This is not to say that this way of thinking is 100 percent accurate 100 percent of the time, but it can give added power to our way of being in community. The question to begin to reclaim our power as citizens is, "If you believed this to be true, in what ways would that make a difference, or change your actions?"

This means that the possibility of an alternative future centers on the question, "Have we chosen the present or has it been handed to us?" The default culture would have us believe that the past creates the future, that a change in individuals causes a change in organizations and community, and that people in authority create people in a subordinate position. That we are determined by everything aside from free will. That culture, history, genetics, organizations, and society drive our actions and our way of being.

All this is true, but the opposite is also true.

The shift toward citizenship is to take the stance that we are the creators of our world as well as the products of it. Free will trumps genetics, culture, and parental upbringing.

The Utility of This Inversion

The first inversion I ran into years ago was the thought that the inmates run the prison. I was skeptical until I worked with some corrections people, who said there is truth in this. Here are some implications of switching our thinking this way:

Inversion: The audience creates the performance.

Implications: Redesign the audience experience. Stop putting so much energy in the talent and message of those on stage. Limit PowerPoint presentations to four slides. Peter Brook immersed the stage in the center of the audience; John Cage held concerts where the rumbling, coughing sounds of the audience *were the show.* When we meet, make it possible for the audience to be engaged with one another. Every auditorium, almost every church, almost every conference room and classroom would be redesigned. Chairs would be mobile; the audience would have sight of one another and know that no matter what occurred onstage, they would not be alone.

Inversion: The subordinate creates the boss.

Implications: Learning, development, and goal setting are in the hands of the subordinate. We would stop doing surveys about how people feel about their bosses, the results of which no one knows what to do with anyway. The attention would turn from the boss to peers, which is the relationship that produces the work.

Inversion: The child creates the parent.

Implications: Parents could sleep through the night. The conversation and industry of inculcating values and forcing consequences onto kids would quiet down. We would focus on the gifts, teachings, and blessings of the young instead of seeing them as problems to be managed. We would listen to them instead of instructing and teaching them again and again. This would allow parents to relax their jaws and index fingers, a secondary health benefit.

Inversion: The citizen creates its leaders.

Implications: Our dependency and disappointment about leaders would go down. The media would have to change their thinking about lead stories. What citizens are doing to improve their community would no longer be human-interest stories but actual news. The cost of elections would be reduced by 90 percent, for the question of whom we elect would be less critical. Candidates for elected office could be poor.

Above all, our leaders would be conveners, not role models and containers for our projections. More on this later.

Inversion: A room and a building are created by the way they are occupied.

Implications: We would be intentional about how we show up. We would spend time designing how we sit in the room, and not be mere consumers of the way the room was intended to be used, or dependent on what the custodians or last group using the room had in mind.

We would redesign the physical space around us—rooms, hallways, reception areas—in a way that affirmed community, so that it had a welcoming feeling and gave the sense that you had come to the right place. Most of all, what we inherited would be a serious subject of discussion.

Inversion: The student creates the teacher and the learning.

Implications: Education would be designed more for learning than for teaching. (This already occurs in many places under the heading of individualized learning. Montessori education has forever operated along these lines.) The social contract in the classroom would be renegotiated toward a partnership between teacher and student. Students would set goals for themselves and be responsible for the learning of other students. Simple ideas, powerful ideas, still rare in practice.

Inversion: Youth create adults.

Implications: Adultism would be confronted. Adults would decide to get interested in the experience of youth instead of always instructing them. When there were meetings and conferences about youth, the voices of youth would be central to the conversation. Youth would become a possibility, not a problem. If we really believed this, we would move our belief in the next generation from lip service to pervasive practice.

Inversion: The listening creates the speaker.

Implications: Listening would be considered an action step. For most of us, listening is just waiting until we get a chance to speak. There might even be a period of silence between statements, and this silence would be experienced as part of the conversation, not dead space. We would also learn what speaking into the listening of the room means. Once again, we would treat the listening as more important than the speaking.

You get the point—the list could go on. In each case, when we invert our thinking, the focus of attention and effort gets redirected.

The power in each of these shifts is that it confronts us with our own freedom. It is out of this freedom, which all of us have ways of escaping, that authentic accountability is born. I will be accountable for only that which I have had a hand in creating, my life and community included.

The inversion of cause refocuses my attention from that person in authority—leader, performer, parent, warden—to that person who together with others also holds the real power. Not to overdo this perspective, for leader, performer, parent, warden are critical partners in community; it's just that they are not the primary or sole proprietors we have construed them to be. We will never eliminate our need for great leaders and people on the stage; we just cannot afford to put all our experience and future in their hands.

• • •

There is no need to argue about this idea of inversion, only to play with its utility. It may not be true, but it is useful in the way it gives us power to evoke the kind of citizen we have defined as crucial to a true community.

Anyone who works in the civic arena has a certain cynicism about citizens. For example, they talk about how hard it is to get parents involved in their child's school. How few people show up at council and board meetings unless they are angry. How such a small number of people are really active in their community. There is truth to this view; it is not just cynicism, it is pretty accurate observation. What restores community is to believe that we play a role in constructing this condition. It is not in the nature of people to be apathetic, entitled, and complainers.

To state the issue simply, as long as we see leader as cause, we will produce passive, entitled citizens. We will put our attention, our training, and our resources wherever we think cause resides. When we see citizen as cause, then this will shift our attention and our wealth, and the energy and creativity that go with it.

This way of thinking takes back our projections and labeling of "others." Plus it counters the expectation that authority figures are essential and central—which not only disempowers students, citizens, audience, but also is a weight too heavy for leaders to carry.

This shift in thinking about cause and effect creates the conditions for a shift in context. The larger import in this line of thinking is that in each case, choice and destiny replace accident and fate. No small thing.

A Word About Entitlement and Accountability

One cost of the retributive conversation is that it breeds entitlement. Entitlement is essentially the conversation, "What's in it for me?" It expresses a scarcity mentality, and the economist tells us that only what is scarce has value. Entitlement is the outcome of a patriarchal culture, which I have discussed too often in other books. But for this discussion, I'll simply say that if we create a context of fear, fault, and retribution, then we will focus on protecting ourselves, which plants the seed of entitlement.

The cost of entitlement is that it is an escape from accountability and soft on commitment. It gets in the way of authentic citizenship.

What is interesting is that the existing public conversation claims to be tough on accountability, but the language of accountability that occurs in a retributive context is code for "control." High-control systems are unbearably soft on accountability. They keep screaming for tighter controls, new laws, and bigger systems, but in the scream, they expose their weakness.

The weakness in the dominant view of accountability is that it thinks people can be *held* accountable. That we can force people to be accountable. Despite the fact that it sells easily, it is an illusion to believe that retribution, incentives, legislation, new standards, and tough consequences will cause accountability.

This illusion is what creates entitlement—and worse, it drives us apart; it does not bring us together. It turns neighbor against neighbor. It denies that we are our brother's keeper. Every colonial and autocratic regime rises to power by turning citizens against each other.

To see our conventional thinking about accountability at work, notice the conversations that dominate our meetings and gatherings. We spend time talking about people not in the room. If not that, our gatherings are designed to sell, change, persuade, and influence others, as if their change will help us reach our goals. These conversations do not produce power; they consume it.

Accountability, Commitment, and the Use of Force

Commitment and accountability are forever paired, for they do not exist without each other. Accountability is the willingness to care for the well-being of the whole; commitment is the willingness to make a promise with no expectation of return.

The economist would say this smacks of altruism, and so be it. What community requires is a promise devoid of barter and not conditional on another's action. Without that, we are constantly in the position of reacting to the choices of others. Which means that our commitment is conditional. This is barter, not commitment.

The cost of constantly reacting to the choices of others is increased cynicism and helplessness. The ultimate cost of cynicism and helplessness is that we resort to the use of force. In this way the barter mentality that dominates our culture helps create a proliferation of force. Not necessarily violence, but the belief that for anything to change, we must mandate or use coercion.

The use of force is an end product of retribution, which rejects altruism and a promise made for its own sake. It rejects the idea that virtue is its own reward.

Commitment is the antithesis of entitlement and barter. Unconditional commitment with no thought to "What's in it for me?" is the emotional and relational essence of community. It is what some call integrity; others, "honoring your word."

Commitment is to choose a path for its own sake. This is the essence of power. Mother Teresa got this. When asked why she worked with people one at a time rather than caring more about having impact on a larger scale, she replied, "I was called by faith, not by results." If you want to argue with Mother Teresa, be my guest.

CHAPTER 7

The Transforming Community

Conventional thinking about communal transformation *believes that focusing on large systems, better leaders, clearer goals, and more controls is essential, and that emphasizing speed and scale is critical. The conventional belief is that individual transformation leads to communal transformation. Our explorations to this point lead instead to the understanding that transformation occurs when we focus on the structure of how we gather and the context in which the gatherings take place; when we work hard on getting the questions right; when we choose depth over speed and relatedness over scale. We also believe that problem solving can make things better but cannot change the nature of things.*

Community transformation calls for citizenship that shifts the context from a place of fear and fault, law and oversight, corporation and "systems," and preoccupation with leadership to one of gifts, generosity, and abundance; social fabric and chosen accountability; and associational life and the engagement of citizens. These shifts occur as citizens face each other in conversations of ownership and possibility. To be more specific, leaders are held to three tasks: to shift the context within which people gather, name the debate through powerful questions, and listen rather than advocate, defend, or provide answers.

• • •

The mindset that we can program and problem-solve our way into a vision does not take into account the complexity and relational nature of community. It undervalues the importance of context and the linguistic, conversational nature of community. If we want to see a change in our communities, we must let go of the conventional or received wisdom about how change occurs. This means we reject or at least seriously question the beliefs that communal change will occur in the following circumstances:

- **We count on an aggregation of individual changes.** We have seen this in attempts by large organizations trying to change their culture through large-scale trainings and change efforts. Communities initiate large-scale dialogue programs and book clubs where many are simultaneously reading the same book. No matter how well intentioned, these efforts largely fall short of their goals. Why? Because individual lives are touched, but the organizational culture and the community are unmoved.

  What's missing is that these efforts do not recognize that there is such a thing as a collective body. A shift in community benefits from shifts in individual consciousness but needs a communal connectedness as well, a communal structure of belonging that produces the foundation for the whole system to move. This is why it is so frustrating to create high performance and consciousness in individuals, and in individual institutions, and then find that they have so little impact on the social capital or fabric of the community.

- **We think in terms of scale and speed.** As David Bornstein has so clearly pointed out, something shifts on a large scale only after a long period of small steps, organized around small groups patient enough to learn and experiment and learn again. Speed and scale are the arguments against what individual and communal transformation require. They are a hallmark of the corporate mindset. When we demand more speed and scale, we are making a coded argument against anything important being any different.

- **We stay focused on large systems and top leaders to implement better problem solving, clearer goals and vision, and better controls of the process.** Large system change is a useful way to think, but transforming action is always local, customized, unfolding, and emergent. The role of leaders is not to be better role models or to drive change; their role is to create the structures and experiences that bring citizens together to identify and solve their own issues.

Communal transformation does occur when we accept the following beliefs:

- **We focus on the structure of how we gather and the context in which our gatherings take place.** Collective change occurs when individuals and small diverse groups engage one another in the presence of many others doing the same. It comes from the knowledge that what is occurring in one space is similarly happening in other spaces, especially ones where I do not know what they are doing. This is the value of a network, or even a network of networks, which is today's version of a social movement. It holds that in larger events, structured in small circles, with the certain conversations that I will define later, the faith in restoration is established. All this needs to be followed up with the usual actions and problem solving, but it is in those moments when citizens engage one another, in communion and the witness of others, that something collective shifts.

  Keeping this focus is especially critical when individuals and institutions meet across boundaries. The key is to structure a way of crossing boundaries where people become connected to those they are not used to being in the room with. Every gathering, in its composition and in its structure, has to be an example of the future we want to create. If this is achieved in this gathering, then that future has occurred today and there is nothing to wait for. Pretty Zen.

- **We work hard on getting the questions right.** This begins by realizing that the questions themselves are important, more important than the answers. The primary questions for community transformation are "How do we choose to be together?" and "What do we want to create together?" These are different from the primary questions for individual transformation, which are "How do I choose to be in whatever setting I find myself in?" and "What am I called to do in this world?"

- **We choose depth over speed and relatedness over scale.** The question "What do we want to create together?" is deceptively complicated. It implies a long journey crossing social, class, and institutional boundaries. Depth takes time and the willingness to engage. Belonging requires the courage to set aside our usual notions of action and measuring success by the numbers touched. It also means that while we keep our own point of view, we leave our self-interest at the door and show up to learn rather than to advocate. These are the conditions whereby we find new places where we belong.

To stay with this thinking—that communal transformation is about the structure of gathering, letting the right questions evolve, and going slow with fewer numbers of people than we would like—we have to continue to shed certain conventional notions. For example, the dominant belief is that better or more leadership, programs, funding, expertise, studies, training, and master plans are the way to build community. Unfortunately, trying harder at these things gives us just a little more of what we already have. They are the path to improvement but not transformation.

Better leadership, funding, training, and the like are about fixing a set of symptoms or problems, which is the conventional conversation. What we want to explore is that way of thinking and being in community that allows our good will to make a real difference. These are ways of thinking and being that can help us choose a new context and find more effective ways to improve our structure of belonging.

Choosing Possibility over Problem Solving

Creating a future is different from defining a future. If our goal is to build social capital and to change the way that citizens are engaged with each other, then we have to shift our thinking about the roles that traditional strategy and problem solving take. We talked earlier about valuing gifts and possibility over needs and problems. Now we can be more detailed about what this looks like.

Our typical way of creating a future is by specifying the vision, the goals, and then defining a blueprint to achieve it. This is called a destination strategy for solving problems. Here are the strategic elements of traditional problem solving:

- **Identify a need.** Find a problem, need, or deficiency that we want to fix or improve.

- **Study and analyze the need.** Do research, assemble facts, survey people, organize survey results and data to make a compelling case for change.

- **Search for solutions.** Brainstorm alternatives. Benchmark where others have solved this deficiency. Bring in experts, consultants, academics, former leaders, and ex–public officials to provide good approaches.

- **Establish goals.** Set realistic and achievable goals, based on the vision. Define outcomes, narrow the effort toward results that can be achieved; the quicker and lower the cost the better. Search for the low-hanging fruit. Maybe initiate a pilot project to prove the viability of the strategy. Laminate the vision, mission, and goals to demonstrate the permanence of this intention.

- **Bring others on board.** Sell to key leaders, meet with citizens to define the effort and name the playing field. Enlist organizations and individuals to create an alliance for change. Publicize the burning platform and stress the urgency and the need for quick results. Give wide distribution to the laminate.

- **Implement.** Launch the program and drive it forward. Stay on message and measure at frequent intervals. Hold people accountable for results, fulfilling promises, and showing outcomes. Declare to others how accountable we are.

- **Loop back.** When the world intervenes and creates a bump in the road, begin the problem solving anew, identifying what went wrong and who was responsible, and initiating a clear oversight process so that this will not happen again.

The essence of these classic problem-solving steps is the belief that the way to make a difference in the world is to define problems and needs and then recommend actions to solve those needs. We are all problem solvers, action oriented, and results minded. It is illegal in this culture to leave a meeting without a to-do list. We want measurable outcomes and we want them now. And this all has such face validity that it seems foolish to argue in any way against it.

Also, this way of thinking does indeed work for many things, especially for the material world. It does not work well with human systems or when the desire is to create something out of nothing. In fact, it is this very mindset, one based on clear definition, prediction, and measurement, that prevents anything fundamental from changing. We still believe that in building a community, we are in effect building and operating a clock. Once again, problem solving makes things better, but it cannot change the nature of things. This insight is at the center of all the thinking about complex adaptive systems, emergent design, and the organic and self-regulating nature of the universe.

The limitations of a clockwork strategy for the future can be seen in one of the most popular forms of community problem solving: creating a vision. Most communities have at some point described a vision for themselves—these visions are developed as a way of defining the destination. (The new millennium was a great occasion for this.) These types of visions have value in that they bring many people together for the sake of development and they give form to the optimism we hold for ourselves. But they are limited in the power to transform because they assume that a defined destination can be reached in a linear path from where we are today. This is the fundamental assumption of the problem-solving model.

Most visions are based upon the belief that we know a lot about what constitutes an ideal or healthy community, which is true. There are many wonderful books that describe what a great community looks like. Jane Jacobs crystallized our thinking about the power of street life. Robert Putnam raised our consciousness about the centrality of social capital. John McKnight's work has built wide support for asset-based community development.

A community will take what it believes to be the thinking of people like these to produce a vision for itself, usually working through the city manager's or mayor's leadership or with group of community leaders. Often this produces, in turn, a neighborhood-by-neighborhood master plan for translating that vision into streets, buildings, services, and public spaces. Elected officials, corporate supporters, and public leaders then go on record supporting the vision and plan.

The challenge for community building is this: While visions, plans, and committed top leadership are important, even essential, no clear vision, nor detailed plan, nor committed group leaders have the power to bring this image of the future into existence without the continued engagement and involvement of citizens. In most instances, citizen engagement ends when the plan is in place. The implementation is put in the hands of the professionals. In concept, the master plan provides some parameters for development and the use of space, but in real life it usually is a call to let the arguing begin. For all its utility, it rarely builds interdependence or strengthens the social fabric of a place.

What brings a fresh future into being is citizens who are willing to self-organize. An alternative future needs the investment of citizens—leaders not in top positions—who are willing to pay the economic and emotional price that creating something really new requires.

Therefore, the challenge for every community is not so much to have a vision of what it wants to become, or a plan, or specific timetables. The real challenge is to discover and create the means for engaging citizens that brings a new possibility into being. To state it more precisely, what gives power to communal possibility is the imagination and authorship of citizens led through a process of engagement. This is an organic and relational process. This is what creates a structure of belonging. This is more critical than the vision and the plan.

Example: Covington

In Covington, Kentucky, several city institutions together chose to use civic engagement as a way of developing a strategic plan for its civil servants and citizens. City Manager Jay Fossett, Center for Great Neighborhoods head Tom DiBello, and the head of the local business association, Gina Breyfogle, asked for help with a series of citizen gatherings to create the agenda for the city following the protocol suggested in this book. Under the leadership of Jeff Stec, a very talented local community builder, we invited the citizens of Covington to four public gatherings. Not to advise the leaders, but to define the priorities of the plan and to commit to making the strategic plan work. Five hundred people in a town of 44,000 showed up to do just this. At the end of the process, the city had its strategic plan—and more important, it had the commitment of a significant group of citizens signed up to make the plan work. Plus, perhaps most important, they strengthened the fabric of their community in the process.

Transformation is about altering the nature of our relatedness and changing the nature of our conversation, as in the community-building effort initiated by local leaders and government in Covington. The problem-solving mindset treats relatedness and language as means rather than the end itself. Therefore, it instrumentalizes relatedness and conversation, keeping problem solving the point.

What creates an alternative future is acting on the belief that context, relatedness, and language are the point, and that traditional problem solving needs to be subordinated and postponed until context, relatedness, and language have shifted. In this thinking, problem solving becomes a means, and not an end in itself.

We cannot problem-solve our way into fundamental change, or transformation, or community. To state it one more way: This is not an argument against problem solving; it is an assertion that the primary work is to shift the context and language and thinking about possibility within which problem solving takes place.

Problem solving leads to an alternative future only when it is embedded in a restorative context, one based on relatedness, generosity, and a focus on gifts. These are the conditions for a new possibility and a shift to shared accountability, and this is what creates a chance for authentic communal transformation. This shift requires us to change our idea of what constitutes action, so that what was once seen as a means to an end now is valued itself as action. Another key insight from Jim Keene, who has spent his life in the public arena, is, "Perhaps the purpose of problems is to give us an excuse to come together."

Expanding Our Idea of Action

Of course, just coming together has to provide some movement toward the future. Every time we meet, we want to feel that we have moved the action forward.

The question is, what qualifies as action? Traditionally, we want a strategy, and a list of next steps and milestones, and the knowledge of who will be responsible for them in order to be satisfied that we have spent our time well when we are together. Any change in the world will, in fact, need this kind of action. To say, however, that this is all that counts as action is too narrow.

If we are to value building social fabric and belonging as much as budgets, timetables, and bricks and mortar, we need to consider action in a broader way. For example:

Would a meeting be worthwhile if we simply strengthened our relationship?

Would a meeting be worthwhile if we learned something of value?

Suppose in a meeting we simply stated our requests of each other and what we were willing to offer each other. Would that justify our time together?

Or, in the gathering, what if we only discussed the gifts we wanted to bring to bear on the concern that brought us together. Would that be an outcome of value?

Saying yes to these questions opens and widens the spectrum of what constitutes action, and this is the point. Relatedness, learning, requests, and offers of gifts are outcomes as valuable as agreements and next steps.

It is not that we are gathering just for the sake of gathering. Or gathering to get to know each other. We come together for an exchange of value and to experience how relatedness, gifts, learning, and generosity are valuable to community. When we name these as outcomes, it allows us to get completion for the investment we made without having to leave with a list for the future.

With this expanded notion of action, we can bring visioning, problem solving, and clearly defined outcomes into the room—and in fact we need them to sustain us. People will meet to learn and connect for only so long, and then a task is needed. The task doesn't have to be the main point of the gathering, but it is an essential point.

PART TWO

The Alchemy of Belonging

Certain properties of collective transformation create the conditions for greater belonging and stronger social fabric. Not that transformation can be reduced to a recipe or set of steps, but its properties can be seen as a combination of ingredients that give it a more concrete structure. Our attempt to convert lead into gold, as with the original alchemists, is part working with the right properties and part an act of faith and spirit.

> To gain the kingdom of heaven is to hear what is not said, to see what cannot be seen, and to know the unknowable.
>
> Hawaiian Queen Liliuokalani to her daughter, after she saw the end of her monarchy

Up to this point, we have said that transformation occurs when we shift context and value possibility, and this grows from a sense of belonging. We can now be specific about the means for making this happen. The following are the properties, in Christopher Alexander's terms, that, when undertaken with a consciousness of the whole, can produce a new future:

Leadership is convening.

The small group is the unit of transformation.

Questions are more transforming than answers.

Six conversations materialize belonging.

Hospitality, the welcoming of strangers, is central.

Physical and social space support belonging.

These provide the framework for the discussion of methodologies that put the ideas from Part One into practice.

CHAPTER 8

Leadership Is Convening

This is not an argument against leaders or leadership, only a desire to change the nature of our thinking. Communal transformation requires a certain kind of leadership, one that creates conditions where context shifts:

- *From a place of fear and fault to one of gifts, generosity, and abundance*
- *From a belief in more laws and oversight to a belief in social fabric and chosen accountability*
- *From the corporation and systems as central, to associational life as central*
- *From a focus on leaders to a focus on citizens*
- *From problems to possibility*

For this shift in context to occur, we need leadership that supports a restorative path. Restoration calls for us to deglamorize leadership and consider it a quality that exists in all human beings. We need to simplify leadership and construct it so that it is infinitely and universally available.

• • •

In communal transformation, leadership is about intention, convening, valuing relatedness, and presenting choices. It is not a personality characteristic or a matter of style, and therefore it requires nothing more than what all of us already have.

This means we can stop looking for leadership as though it were scarce or lost, or it had to be trained into us by experts. If our traditional form of leadership has been studied for so long, written about with such admiration, defined by so many, worshipped by so few, and the cause of so much disappointment, maybe doing more of all that is not productive. The search for great leadership is a prime example of how we too often take something that does not work and try harder at it.

I have written elsewhere about reconstructing *leader* as social architect. Not leader as special person, but leader as a citizen willing to do those things that have the capacity to initiate something new in the world. In this way, leader belongs right up there with cook, carpenter, artist, and landscape designer. It is a capacity that can be learned by all of us, with a small amount of teaching and an agreement to practice. The ultimate do-it-yourself movement.

Community building requires a concept of the leader as one who creates experiences for others—experiences that in themselves are examples of our desired future. The experiences we create need to be designed in such a way that relatedness, accountability, and commitment are every moment available, experienced, and demonstrated. David Isaacs of the World Café calls this "relational leadership."

This concept of leadership means that in addition to embracing their own humanity, which is the work of every person, the core task of leaders is to create the conditions for civic or institutional engagement. They do this through the power they have to name the debate and design gatherings. We use the term *gathering*, because the word has different associations from what we think of when we say "meeting." Most people do not even like meetings, and for good reason. They are frequently designed to explain, defend, express opinions, persuade, set more goals, and define steps—the result of which is to produce more of what currently exists. These kinds of meetings either review the past or embody the belief that better planning, better managing, or more measurement and prediction can create an alternative future. So the word *gathering* is intended to distinguish what we are talking about here, something with more significance than the common sense of *meeting*.

Engagement Is the Point

Leadership begins with understanding that every gathering is an opportunity to deepen accountability and commitment through engagement. It doesn't matter what the stated purpose of the gathering is.

Each gathering serves two functions: to address its stated purpose, its business issues; and to be an occasion for each person to decide to become engaged as an owner. The leader's task is to structure the place and experience of these occasions to move the culture toward shared ownership.

This is very different from the conventional belief that the task of leadership is to set a vision, enroll others in it, and hold people accountable through measurements and reward. Consider how most current leadership trainings assert the following:

- Leader and top are essential. They are role models who need to possess a special set of personal skills.

- The task of the leader is to define the destination and the blueprint to get there.

- The leader's work is to bring others on board. Enroll, align, inspire.

- Leaders provide for the oversight, measurement, and training needed (as defined by leaders).

Each of these beliefs elevates leaders as an elite group, singularly worthy of special development, coaching, and incentives. All of these beliefs have face validity, and they have unintended consequences. When we are dissatisfied with a leader, we simply try harder to find a new one who will perform more perfectly in the very way that led to our last disappointment. This creates a level of isolation, entitlement, and passivity that our communities cannot afford to carry.

The world does not need leaders to better define issues, or to orchestrate better planning or project management. What it needs is for the issues and the plans to have more of an impact, and that comes from citizen accountability and commitment. Engagement is the means through which there can be a shift in caring for the well-being of the whole, and the task of leader as convener is to produce that engagement.

The Art of Convening

The shift is to believe that the task of leadership is to provide context and produce engagement, to tend to our social fabric. It is to see the leader as one whose function is to engage groups of people in a way that creates accountability and commitment.

In this way of thinking we hold leadership to three tasks:

- Create a context that nurtures an alternative future, one based on gifts, generosity, accountability, and commitment.
- Initiate and convene conversations that shift people's experience, which occurs through the way people are brought together and the nature of the questions used to engage them.
- Listen and pay attention.

Convening leaders create and manage the social space within which citizens get deeply engaged. Through this engagement, citizens discover that it is in their power to resolve something or at least move the action forward. Engagement, and the accountability that grows out of it, occurs when we ask people to be in charge of their own experience and act on the well-being of the whole. Leaders do this by naming a new context and convening people into new conversations through questions that demand personal investment. This is what triggers the choice to be accountable for those things over which we can have power, even though we may have no control.

• • •

In addition to convening and naming the question, we add listening to the critical role of leadership. Listening may be the single most powerful action the leader can take. Leaders will always be under pressure to speak, but if building social fabric is important, and sustained transformation is the goal, then listening becomes the greater service.

This kind of leadership—convening, naming the question, and listening—is restorative and produces energy rather than consumes it. It is leadership that creates accountability as it confronts people with their freedom. In this way, engagement-centered leaders bring kitchen table and street corner democracy into being.

Example: Findley House

Seven Hills is a neighborhood center in the West End of Cincinnati. One of its locations is called Findley House, and a project there illustrates the power of engagement-centered listening. The story starts when four "leaders" were asked to work with a group of urban youths. The essence of the story is that they resisted the temptation to be helpful.

Joan and Michael Hoxsey and Geralyn and Tom Sparough were four white overeducated adults when they first met with a dozen streetwise African-American youths in what began as an intervention to help the youths, including a full curriculum on what these young men "ought" to learn about relationships.

Shortly into the effort, the Hoxseys and Sparoughs realized that to make any difference in the young men's lives, the adults had to try to understand who these young people were. So they threw out the curriculum and decided to simply hang out with the youths. They listened two nights a week for eight months. The listening was hard, the language was hard, the stories were heartbreaking.

At first it seemed the young men were unreachable, and any attempt to "help" would be futile. Then, at some point the adults' listening made a difference. The adults and the young people began to trust one another. As one young man put it, "The reason I respect you so much is because you may be the only people who really listen. Everyone wanted to tell us to 'pull up our pants' and tell us how to live." Something valuable was built, and in the end the "things" the adults wanted to teach about relationships were taught by simply changing the nature of the conversation.

In this same facility, there were two other programs for the youth started at the same time: GED training and computer skills training. Both of these programs had something in mind for the young men, something the leadership knew was best for them. By the end of this part of the program, the youths simply stopped showing up. Operating under the traditional ideas of good leadership, the GED program and the computer training program were gone. The youths rejected that kind of help.

Even when the program that brought the youths and the Hoxseys and Sparoughs together ended, these adults and youths continued to meet, and they are all currently working on a longer-term project: making a movie about the crucible of choices facing young urban people. What turned out to be sustainable and durable over time is the program of listening and valuing run by the Hoxseys and Sparoughs, whom the youths decided to trust.

One of the challenges facing relational approaches such as this is that they do not measure well. If we were to take a conventional approach to measuring these efforts, we would look for computer skill improvement and how many got their GED diplomas. The report would give low marks to the easily measured expected outcomes. We would probably conclude that the youths were not ready to learn. We would not consider the computer and GED efforts a failure in leadership—that would be too strong an indictment of our current thinking.

The social outcomes of the Hoxseys' and Sparoughs' work would most likely not be valued by the assessment at all, nor would their leadership style show up as a positive factor. Conventional measures would miss the essence of the humanity and restraint that led to transformation in the form of a group of young African-Americans finding four white people, in positions of leadership, whom they could trust.

The Convening Capacity of Elected Officials

Elected officials are a special case of how we think about leadership and the art of convening. We have put elected officials in a difficult role. We distort them into service providers and suppliers. We relate to them as if we are consumers, not citizens. We want them to solve *for* us those issues that we should be solving for ourselves.

The customer model, in which elected officials exist to satisfy citizen demands, is a disservice to community, even though citizens love it. Elected officials are partners with citizens, not suppliers. The most useful role that elected officials can perform is to bring citizens together. They have this convening capacity like no one else in a city, but it is way underutilized. If elected officials take on this role as their primary one, we may still occasionally request that they pass some legislation or ordinance that serves us, but this should be the exception. If we continue to define elected officials primarily as legislators, then we are going to have to endure the results of their productivity.

Example: Cold Spring

Mark Stoeber is the mayor of Cold Spring, Kentucky, a small and mostly residential town. At some point he realized that the citizen complaints he was getting did not need an elected official to resolve. For example, he was getting complaints in one neighborhood about someone's dog. Mark decided that the complaint about the dog was a symptom of the lack of connectedness among neighbors. With the dog's behavior as cover, he asked one citizen to host a meeting in their home with other neighbors. Neighbors showed up, including the dog owner, and an agreement was reached. Social fabric became a little stronger. The mayor moved on to other things.

A year later, Mark decided to take another step and invited about 20 community leaders into a conversation with city council members. They met in council chambers, but not in the usual configuration. In Cold Spring, as in most cities, the council sits on a platform and citizens sit in seats on a lower level. For this meeting, everyone sat in chairs in circles at the same level in the council room. They arranged themselves in groups to sit with people they knew the least and talked about some of the questions we are discussing here: crossroads facing the town, the major gifts of the town and its citizens, doubts about anything really shifting, a look at the future demands facing the town, and what commitment they had to participate in engaging more people to develop the possibility called Cold Spring.

A small but symbolic beginning for an elected official deciding that the future economic development and quality of life of the town were dependent on the quality of relatedness of its citizens and its ability to bring those on the margin into the center.

Local government has two primary responsibilities. One is to sustain and improve the infrastructure of its community: roads, traffic, transportation, public safety, code enforcement, economic development, master planning, environment, and more. City managers and civil servants are well trained to do this and mostly do an excellent job at it.

The other role of local government is to build the social fabric of the community. They are in a key position to engage citizens in the well-being of the city. The challenge in doing this is enlarged by the structures they most often use to do it. The typical forms of engagement are city council meetings, public hearings, neighborhood summits, town hall meetings, and any variety of speaking engagements and special events that they attend.

There is nothing in the current structure of these gatherings that encourages citizens to get connected to each other or to be engaged as producers of the future. Citizens show up as critics and consumers.

For local government to build social fabric and create the context for a restorative community, the form in which citizens are involved needs to change from a patriarchal, consumer model to a partnership model that takes advantage of the energizing power of the small group.

CHAPTER 9

The Small Group Is
the Unit of Transformation

The future is created one room at a time, one gathering at a time. Each gathering needs to become an example of the future we want to create. This means the small group is where transformation takes place. Large-scale transformation occurs when enough small group shifts lead to the larger change. Small groups have the most leverage when they meet as part of a larger gathering. At these moments, citizens experience the intimacy of the small circle and are simultaneously aware that they are part of a larger whole that shares their concerns.

The small group gains power with certain kinds of conversations. To build community, we seek conversations where people show up by invitation rather than mandate, and experience an intimate and authentic relatedness. We have conversations where the focus is on the communal possibility and there is a shift in ownership of this place, even though others are in charge. We structure these conversations so that diversity of thinking and dissent are given space, commitments are made without barter, and the gifts of each person and our community are acknowledged and valued.

• • •

Communal transformation is best initiated through those times when we gather. It is when groups of people are in a room together that a shift in context is noticed, felt, and reinforced. This means that each gathering takes on a special importance as a leading indicator of the future. Every meeting or special event is that place where context can be shifted, relatedness can be built, and new conversation can be introduced. The times that we gather is when we draw conclusions about what kind of community we live in.

We change the world one room at a time. This room, today, becomes an example of the future we want to create. There is no need to wait for the future. Creating the experience of belonging in the room we are in at the moment becomes the point, namely that the way we structure the assembly of peers and leaders is as critical as the issue or future we come together to address.

One conventional structure for meeting is described in *Robert's Rules of Order*. It is good at efficiency and containing conflict; it is also good at dampening energy. Even when *Robert's Rules* do not apply, which is most of the time, our meetings typically pay primary attention to explanation, persuasion, and problem solving, rather than engagement, and in this way they also drain our aliveness. For community building, we want to give as much or more attention to that which creates energy as we give to the content, which usually exhausts energy.

Creating energy is critical, for in our gatherings we have the most control and influence over shifting the context and public conversation. It is true that other factors, such as the media message and the policy stance of public figures, make a difference. The media has a large impact on the narrative of our community and our experience of it. Public policy can make what we do easier or more difficult. However, most citizens who want an alternative future, including some of the community's leaders, have little short-term control over these factors. When there is a shift in the way citizens listen and speak, however, then the context spoken by the media and the stance of public figures will shift, hope will be generated, and energy released.

Therefore, like it or not, the way we design our gatherings is the only way we can bring into existence the possibility of the community we want to inhabit. Everything that occurs outside the room we are in at the moment is an abstraction and leads us into conversations of complaint and wishful thinking.

The Power of the Small Group

All change includes work in one or more small groups, which is why we use the shorthand phrase "The small group is the unit of transformation." The small group is the structure that allows every voice to be heard. It is in groups of 3 to 12 that intimacy is created. This intimate conversation makes the process personal. It provides the structure where people overcome isolation and where the experience of belonging is created. Even though we may be in a room filled with a large number of people we will never meet, by having made intimate contact with a handful of people in our small group work we are brought into connection with all others.

The small group is the bridge between our own individual existence and the larger community. In the small group discussion we discover that our own concerns are more universal than we imagined. This discovery that we are not alone, that others can at least understand what is on our mind, if not agree with us, is what creates the feeling of belonging. When this occurs in the same place and time, in the presence of a larger community, the collective possibility begins to take form and have legs.

The power of the small group cannot be overemphasized. Something almost mystical, certainly mysterious, occurs when citizens sit in a small group, for they often become more authentic and personal with each other there than in other settings. Designing small group conversations (more about that later) is so simple that it rarely receives the attention and importance it deserves.

The small group also offers a self-correcting quality when things are not going well. There are always times in any gathering when we become stuck. Energy is low, perhaps there is anger or cynicism in the room, or simply confusion, and we are unsure what to do. The best path in nearly every situation is to put our faith in citizens to identify and name what is occurring. Simply request people to form small groups of three or four and ask them to discuss what is going on and report back in ten minutes. This request need not be sophisticated. Simply say, "Form small groups of four and talk about how this meeting is going and to what extent we are getting what we came for."

In doing this, we ask the community to take responsibility for the success of this gathering and express faith in their good will, even if they are frustrated with what is happening. This act is a way of shifting power and accountability from leader to citizens; and in most cases, citizens will identify what needs to occur to get the action back on track. Doing this is an acknowledgment that critical wisdom resides in the community.

The point is that every large group meeting needs to use small groups to create connection and move the action forward. As obvious as this might seem, it amazes me how many events and gatherings do not do this. How many conferences, summits, and events have we attended where the small group discussion is relegated to the breaks and thereby left to chance?

The Role of the Large Group

In gatherings where there are more than 20 people in the room—which I am calling the large group—we need to move back and forth from the small group to the large group. Same if there are a thousand in the room. There have to be moments when the whole room hears individual voices and what other small groups are speaking about. Holding to the metaphoric meaning of "the room as a microcosm of the universe," when people share with a larger group, they are sharing with the world.

These are the moments where individuals have an opportunity to stand for something. So, as a symbol of the larger purpose of the gathering, a person speaking to the whole literally needs to physically stand. As they "stand" for something for themselves, they are standing for the sake of all in the room. As each person stands, we ask their name so they can be known for their stance.

A place of belonging is one where all voices have value, so we need to make sure that citizen voices receive the same technological boost as leaders'. When people speak to the large group, their voices need to be amplified so that all can hear. Our belief in the importance of the voices of citizens hinges on what may seem like a secondary matter: the availability of a microphone for all who choose to speak.

Having a standing microphone for citizens that they have to walk to and even line up behind does not count. Most public meetings have leaders with their own mikes and citizens traveling to a common mike. The geography of this disparity speaks volumes as to who is important (leader) and therefore who has the future in their hands. Juanita Brown and David Isaacs have written the profound insight that every moment is a combination of methodology and metaphor. What may seem like a small procedural or technological matter is actually much more important than we have imagined because of its metaphoric message. The amplification of a human voice is a good example of this.

What has slowly dawned on me over time is that the outcome of small and large group experiences is primarily determined by a set of details that I thought were incidental, as in the example mentioned above: people standing when they speak, the voice amplified so that the sound of the citizen is as clear as the sound of a leader.

Another example: Ask people making a powerful statement to the whole community to say it again slowly. They speak for all others who are silent, and in that way they speak for the whole. These can be sacred moments and repetition honors this. One more detail along these lines: When people speak in a large group, they need to be acknowledged for the courage it took to speak out.

Most of this way of being in groups is part of the emerging but well-established methodology often called *large group interventions*. These were noted in the first chapter. The intent throughout this book is to bring what has been facilitator technique into everyday practice, and to underline the potential power of these practices.

Example: The Hawaiian Democratic Party

Mike McCartney is a long-time leader in the Democratic Party in Hawaii. His commitment is to change the nature of the political debate there. His way of combining metaphor and methodology is to reframe elected officials as servant leaders and shift the conversation from problems and partisanship to the well-being of the whole community. Another leader who understands this is Jimmy Toyama. Before he got the job as the chair of the Democratic Party in Honolulu, Jimmy held a wider vision of the role a political party can play in society. To say that its main purpose is to win elections was too small a purpose. Jimmy held a series of conferences to create the conversation of possibility for the Democratic Party. They held conversations of gifts, ownership, and commitment . . . in small groups, with those they knew least. So simple, but very different from the usual party meeting.

Conversations That Count

Mike and Jimmy's work with the Hawaiian Democratic Party is partly an illustration of the structure and importance of groups, and partly, and more important, a way to bring us to the content of the conversations that can produce the context and future we seek.

To say that the future is dependent on having conversations we have not had before does not mean that *any* new conversation will make a difference. So what specific kinds of conversations can create the relatedness and accountability that are the heart of a restorative context?

To create a community of accountability and belonging, we seek conversations where the following is true:

An intimate and authentic *relatedness* is experienced.

The world is shifted through *invitation* rather than mandate.

The focus is on the communal *possibility*.

There is a shift in *ownership* of this place, even though others are in charge.

Diversity of thinking and *dissent* are given space.

Commitments are made without barter.

The *gifts* of each person and our community are acknowledged and valued.

These are the specific conversations that are central to communal transformation. It is when we choose to speak of invitation, possibility, ownership, dissent, commitment, and gifts that transformation occurs. This is the speaking and listening that is the linguistic shift that changes the context through which community can be restored and traditional problem solving and development can make the difference.

There is a great deal written and practiced about creating new conversations, all of which is of great value and holds the same spirit of what will be offered here. Much of what is written is about handling difficult conversations in a way that builds relationships and holding crucial conversations that are important for the success of an organization. There has been for some time an important dialogue movement to help people understand their own mental models and listen more deeply as an act of inquiry.

The types of conversations offered here, and explored in more depth in the next three chapters, are a little different in that they are aimed at building community, whereas many of the others are primarily aimed at individual development or improving relationships. Plus these community-building conversations are pointedly designed to confront the issue of accountability and commitment. That aside, all the movements toward shifting conversation are extremely valuable, and all serve to change the world in a positive way.

Questions Are More Transforming Than Answers

We can now be specific about defining the conversations that open community to an alternative future. We seek conversations that create accountability and commitment. The traditional conversations that seek to explain, study, analyze, define tools, and express the desire to change others are interesting but not powerful. They actually are forms of wanting to maintain control. If we adhere to them, they become a limitation to the future, not a pathway.

The future is brought into the present when citizens engage each other through questions of possibility, commitment, dissent, and gifts. Questions open the door to the future and are more powerful than answers in that they demand engagement. Engagement is what creates accountability. How we frame the questions is decisive. They need to be ambiguous, personal, and stressful. The way we introduce the questions also matters. We name the distinction the question addresses by stating what is different and unique about this conversation. We give permission for unpopular answers, and inoculate people against advice and help. Advice is replaced by curiosity.

• • •

Transformation and restoration occur through the power of language, and how we speak and listen to each other. This is the medium through which a more positive future is created or denied. Nice theory, but operationally how does this occur? What is the means to achieve the full impact of this idea?

We begin by realizing, at a basic level, that we need a new conversation. Some will say we are already having these conversations. Maybe, but even if ownership, dissent, gifts, commitment, and possibility are on the agenda, they are rarely pursued in a way that causes a real shift. We need to identify a way to hold these conversations so that the chance of creating something new increases, so that they have the quality of aliveness we seek.

The conversation is not so much about the future for the community, but is the future itself. A parallel way to think of this is to consider the meaning of a yoga practice. Anyone beginning yoga struggles with the postures and cannot help but feel inadequate, have doubts about their body, and think the purpose of the practice is the core strength and flexibility it produces, or not. We are told—and sometimes get—that even the way we breathe can be a pathway to a better life.

All this is true, but the larger insight, the meta-goal, is to realize that "how you do the mat is how you do your life." That the practice of yoga itself is your life. Creating good postures, breathing, and flexibility are simply fringe benefits. It is your way of doing the practice itself that is the breakthrough, not some future moment in which a better state of being is accomplished. This way there is nothing to wait for, no future or objective measure of accomplishment to be attained.

The same with certain conversations. Holding them in a restorative context—one of possibility, generosity, and gifts, in relationship with others—is as much the transformation as any place that those conversations might lead you. The right small group conversation releases aliveness and intention into the community. This creates the condition where the symptoms and fragmentation and breakdown can be healed. It is only within this context and communal aliveness that our skill at problem solving will make the difference.

The community does not shift by having any new conversation. Nothing will change if the new conversation is a discussion about better language, or if we work harder on analyzing or explaining the issue at hand. Studying, trying harder to understand, seeking better programs or tools—these have no power. They are only interesting. Without a conversation that has accountability built into it, we may build relatedness and the room may become gentler, but the community and how it constructs itself do not shift.

Conversations that evoke accountability and commitment can best be produced through deciding to value *questions* more than answers, by choosing to put as much thought into questions as we have traditionally given to answers.

The Construction of Questions

Questions are more transformative than answers and are the essential tools of engagement. They are the means by which we are all confronted with our freedom. In this sense, if you want to change the context, find powerful questions.

Questions create the space for something new to emerge. Answers, especially those that respond to our need for quick results, while satisfying, shut down the discussion, and the future shuts down with them. Most leaders are well schooled in providing answers and remain rather indifferent and naive as far as the use of questions goes. How many PowerPoint presentations have you seen flooded with answers, blueprints, analyses, and proposals? How many have you seen presenting questions?

What makes us impatient with questions and hungry for answers is that we confuse exploring a question with talk that has no meaning—argument, analysis, explanation, and defense—talk that leaves us despairing about citizens coming together to create something. Questions that trigger argument, analysis, explanation, and defense have little power. They may be interesting, but that is different from being powerful.

The shift in public conversation toward powerful questions is what, in our terms, constitutes transforming action.

A reminder: Questions alone are not enough. Context matters. The mindset of how people came to be in the room matters. The room itself matters. The social structure of how people talk to each other matters. The action of the leader/convener matters. But for this moment, let us stay with the questions.

Powerful questions are those that, in the answering, evoke a choice for accountability and commitment. They are questions that take us to requests, offers, declarations, forgiveness, confession, gratitude, and welcome, all of which are memorable and have a transformative power.

> Questions are fateful. They determine destinations. They are the chamber through which destiny calls.
>
> Godwin Hlatshwayo

Without strong questions, we collude with people who might attend a gathering and choose not to join in cocreating the value of the event. The point is that the nature of the questions we ask either keeps the existing system in place or brings an alternative future into the room. So I want to distinguish in more detail between questions that have little and great power.

Questions with Little Power

The existing conversation is organized around a set of traditional questions that have little power to create an alternative future. These are the questions the world is constantly asking. It is understandable that we ask them, but they carry no power; and in the asking, each of these questions is an obstacle to addressing what has given rise to the question in the first place:

How do we get people to show up and be committed?

How do we get others to be more responsible?

How do we get people to come on board and to do the right thing?

How do we hold those people accountable?

How do we get others to buy in to our vision?

How do we get those people to change?

How much will it cost and where do we get the money?

How do we negotiate for something better?

What new policy or legislation will move our interests forward?

Where is it working? Who has solved this elsewhere and how do we import that knowledge?

How do we find and develop better leaders?

Why aren't those people in the room?

If we answer these questions directly, from the context from which they are asked, we are supporting the mindset that an alternative future can be negotiated, mandated, engineered, and controlled into existence. They call us to try harder at what we have been doing.

The hidden agenda in these questions is to maintain dominance and to be right. They urge us to raise standards, measure more closely, and return to basics, purportedly to create accountability. They are not really about returning to basics, they are about returning to what got us here. These questions have no power; they only carry force.

All these questions preserve innocence for the one asking. They imply that the one asking knows, and other people are a problem to be solved. These are each an expression of reliance on the use of force to make a difference in the world. They occur when we lose faith in our own power and the power of our community.

Questions that are designed to change other people are the wrong questions. Wrong, not because they don't matter or are based on ill intent, but wrong because they reinforce the problem-solving model. They are questions that are the cause of the very thing we are trying to shift: the fragmented and retributive nature of our communities. The conversations about standards, measures, and the change needed in others destroy relatedness, and it is in this way that they work against belonging and community.

These questions are also a response to the wish to create a predictable future. We want desperately to take uncertainty out of the future. But when we take uncertainty out, it is no longer the future. It is the present projected forward. Nothing new can come from the desire for a predictable tomorrow. The only way to make tomorrow predictable is to make it just like today. In fact, what distinguishes the future is its unpredictability and mystery.

Questions with Great Power

Questions that have the power to make a difference are ones that engage people in an intimate way, confront them with their freedom, and invite them to cocreate a future possibility.

Achieving accountability and commitment entails the use of questions through which, in the act of answering them, we become cocreators of the world. It does not matter what our answers to the questions are. The questions have an impact even if the response is to refuse to answer them. To state it more dramatically: Powerful questions are the ones that cause you to become an actor as soon as you answer them. You no longer have the luxury of being a spectator of whatever it is you are concerned about. Regardless of how you answer these questions, you are guilty. Guilty of having created this world. Not a pleasant thought, but the moment we accept the idea that we have created the world, we have the power to change it.

Powerful questions also express the reality that change, like life, is difficult and unpredictable. They open up the conversation—in contrast to questions that are, in a sense, answers in disguise. Answers in disguise narrow and control the dialogue, and thereby the future.

We can generalize what qualities define great questions, and this gives us the capacity not just to remember a list but also to create powerful questions of our own.

A great question has three qualities:

It is ambiguous. There is no attempt to try to precisely define what is meant by the question. This requires each person to bring their own, personal meaning into the room.

It is personal. All passion, commitment, and connection grow out of what is most personal. We need to create space for the personal.

It evokes anxiety. All that matters makes us anxious. It is our wish to escape from anxiety that steals our aliveness. If there is no edge to the question, there is no power.

Questions themselves are an art form worthy of a lifetime of study. They are what transform the hour. Here are some questions that have the capacity to open the space for a different future:

What is the commitment you hold that brought you into this room?

What is the price you or others pay for being here today?

How valuable do you plan for this effort to be?

What is the crossroads you face at this stage of the game?

What is the story you keep telling about the problems of this community?

What are the gifts you hold that have not been brought fully into the world?

What is your contribution to the very thing you complain about?

What is it about you or your team, group, or neighborhood that no one knows?

These questions have the capacity to move something forward, and we will explore them—and others—in more depth in the coming chapters. By answering these kinds of questions, we become more accountable, more committed, more vulnerable; and when we voice our answers to one another, we grow more intimate and connected.

The Setup Is Everything

Once we have a question, there is a way of setting up the conversation that makes a big difference. Context is decisive at every level. If the conversation is not set up clearly and intentionally, the old conversation will occur. To initiate a new conversation, we have to give a reason for it, and we have to warn people against bringing forth the limitations of the old conversation—namely, to guard against solution finding and advice giving.

The setup is as important as the question, for it provides the context. As a reminder, the context we are creating space for is relatedness, accountability, gifts, and generosity. Being precise about the setup is an essential task of leadership. Without a clear setup, each and every time, citizens will revert to the default conversation. The setup inoculates us against the power and habit of speaking into scarcity and dependency. It is so seductive to start talking about the need for more funding, the wish for better leadership, the power of the media, and how others need to change.

There are four elements to the setup:

- Name the distinctions.
- Give permission for unpopular answers.
- Avoid advice and replace it with curiosity.
- Precisely name the question.

Name Distinctions

Each question has a quality that distinguishes it from the default mindset. Making this distinction clear is critical. For example, if we want to confront people's willingness to join us as owners of this gathering, we ask, "How valuable an experience do you *plan* to have in this event?" This is distinguished from the question "How valuable an experience do you *want* to have?" or "How valuable an experience do you *think* it will be?" The distinction between "plan" and "want" or "think" is the difference between choice and wishful thinking or prediction. *Wanting* to have a good experience does not mean we choose it. We can make a *prediction* about how valuable the experience will be, but this puts us in the position of waiting to see what the world will provide us.

There is no power in wanting or predicting; the power is in deciding. Even if we say that we plan for this experience to be of no value, we have taken the stance of ownership. What is so difficult to communicate is that ownership is more important than results. If I say that I plan for something to not be valuable, I have shown up as an owner, and that is what brings an alternative future into being. The instant I show up as an owner, I have reclaimed my place as a creator and participant in community.

To ask what kind of experience we *plan* to have places the ownership of that experience clearly in our own hands. The language of what we plan requires us to be accountable.

Every community-building question is about creating a powerful distinction as in the ownership example, and every time the distinction needs to be named. In every conversation the issue is the same: moving toward choice and accountability for the well-being of the whole. In the case of ownership, the distinction is between planning and wanting/predicting. If we are not aware of the distinction that makes the question powerful, we shouldn't use the question.

Give Permission for Unpopular Answers

When people are asked a question, they are conditioned to seek the right answer to feel good, or to fit in for the sake of belonging. Encourage them to answer honestly, by naming possible unpopular answers and supporting their expression.

For example, on the ownership question, let them know that an answer that says they plan for this to be a very poor experience is a fine one. Literally say, "If you plan for this meeting to be a waste of time, give it a 1 on a 7-point scale, where 1 is yuck and 7 is wow. It is more important to declare where you are at this moment than for you to demonstrate optimism." All we care about is that people own their experience, not that the experience be a good one.

Create an Advice-Free Zone

We need to tell people not to be helpful. Trying to be helpful and giving advice are really ways to control others. Advice is a conversation stopper. In community building, we want to substitute curiosity for advice. No call to action. No asking what they are going to do about it. Do not tell people how you handled the same concern in the past. Do not ask questions that have advice hidden in them, such as "Have you ever thought of talking to the person directly?"

Often citizens will ask for advice. The request for advice is how we surrender our sovereignty. If we give in to this request, we have, in this small instance, affirmed their servitude, their belief that they do not have the capacity to create the world from their own resources; and more important, we have supported their escape from their own freedom.

Advice also weakens relatedness, even if people ask for it. Urge citizens to ask one another instead, "Why does that mean so much to you?" When they answer, ask the same question again, "And why does *that* mean so much to you?" The goal is to replace advice with curiosity. The future hinges on this issue. Advice, recommendations, and obvious actions are exactly what increase the likelihood that tomorrow will be just like yesterday.

> One of the basic elements of the relationship between oppressor and oppressed is prescription. Every prescription represents the imposition of one individual's choice upon another, transforming the consciousness of the person prescribed to into one that conforms with the prescriber's consciousness.
>
> Paolo Freire, *The Pedagogy of the Oppressed*

The Risk Order of Questions

Certain questions require a greater level of trust among citizens than others. A good design begins with less-demanding questions and ends with the more-difficult ones. The conversations of ownership, commitment, and gifts are high risk and require greater trust to have meaning. Discussions of crossroads, possibility, and dissent are easier and come earlier—this should get clearer in the coming chapters.

Example: Possibility over Problem Solving

Phil Cass is a foundation executive in Columbus, Ohio, and is part of a group bringing many of the ideas in this book into the health care debate. He is using a methodology developed in Europe called the Art of Hosting, which is referenced at the end of the book. Phil's strategy is to create a series of community conversations involving a cross-section of several hundred citizens in reimagining and ultimately reforming health care. They understand the importance of the question and how the conversation is framed. The results of those gatherings are profound: The conversation has shifted from how to reform the existing health care system to how to create a system that nurtures the health and well-being of each citizen of that community. The cynic would say it is just semantics; the activist who believes the future is waiting to be created would know that the transformation has begun.

Midterm Review

B efore I make these ideas more concrete, here is a quick over-view of the larger story we are creating:

Powerful questions give us the means to initiate a community where account-ability and commitment are ingrained. They are a key to understanding the means and architecture for gathering people in a way that will build relat-edness, which in turn creates communities in which citizens will choose accountability and commitment. This is what overcomes our fragmenta-tion and reduces our tendency to demand change from people who are essentially strangers to us.

The thinking follows this logic: The strategy for an alternative future is to focus on ways to shift context, build relatedness, and create space for a more intentional possibility.

This strategy gives form to the idea that if you can change context and relatedness in this room, you have changed the context and relatedness in the world, at least for this moment.

The way we change the room is by changing the conversation. Not to just any new conversation, but to one that creates a communal accountability and commitment. And this new conversation is almost always initiated in the form of a question.

We are avoiding conversations that are just talk. Certain conversations are satisfying and true, yet they have no power and entail no accountability.

For example:

Telling the history of how we got here

Giving explanations and opinions

Blaming and complaining

Making reports and descriptions

Carefully defining terms and conditions

Retelling your story again and again

Seeking quick action

These are the conventional conversations and are often conducted through conferences, press releases, trainings, master plans, and the call for more studies and expertise. They are well intentioned and have face validity but don't change anything. Most of what we want to see changed has been explained, complained about, reported on, and defined for decades.

"Just-talk" conversations can help us get connected or increase our understanding of who we are, but we endure them mostly out of habit, for they are so ingrained in the social convention of our culture that if we didn't have them, we would miss it. They do not, however, contribute to transformation. Here are the conversations that produce something more than just talk:

Invitation

Possibility

Ownership

Dissent

Commitment

Gifts

Each of these conversations leads to the others. Any one held wholeheartedly takes us to and resolves all the others. When any of them are absent, it is just talk, no matter how urgent the cause, how important the plan, how elegant the answer. These are the conversations through which the community is transformed.

CHAPTER 11

Invitation

The first of the six conversations that create an accountable and hospitable community is invitation. Once the invitation conversation takes place, we follow with the conversations of possibility, ownership, dissent, commitment, and gifts.

Invitation is the means through which hospitality is created. Invitation counters the conventional belief that change requires mandate or persuasion. Invitation honors the importance of choice, the necessary condition for accountability. We begin with the question of whom do we want in the room. For starters, we want people who are not used to being together. Then we include the six elements of a powerful invitation: naming the possibility about which we are convening, being clear about whom we invite, emphasizing freedom of choice in showing up, specifying what is required of each should they choose to attend, making a clear request, and making the invitation as personal as possible.

• • •

As we enter the conversations for structuring belonging, a caveat: Real life is circuitous; it does not develop the way the conversations appear on a page. Except for the invitation, deciding which conversations to have, in which order, will vary with the context of a gathering. Since all the conversations lead to each other, sequence is not critical. The conversations described here and in the next chapter, though, appear in the rough order that usually aligns with the logic of people's experience.

Conversation One: The Invitation

Hospitality, the welcoming of strangers, is the essence of a restorative community. Historically, if strangers knocked at your door, you automatically invited them in. They would be fed and offered a place to sleep, even if they were your enemies. As long as they were in your house, they were safe from harm. They were treated as if they belonged, regardless of the past. This is the context of restoration we are seeking. Our hospitality begins with the invitation.

The conversation for invitation is the decision to engage other citizens to be part of the possibility that we are committed to. The invitation is in itself an act of generosity, and the mere act of inviting may have more meaning than anything that happens in the gathering.

An invitation is more than just a request to attend; it is a call to create an alternative future, to join in the possibility we have declared. The question is, "What is the invitation we can make for people to participate in creating a future distinct from the past?"

The Distinction for the Invitation Conversation

The distinction here is between invitation and the more typical ways of achieving change: mandate and persuasion. The belief in mandate and persuasion triggers talk about how to change other people and how do we get those people on board, how do we make showing up a requirement, all of which are simply our desire to control others. What is distinct about an invitation is that it can be refused, at no cost to the one refusing.

An authentic invitation operates without promising incentives or rewards. Offering inducements such as door prizes, gifts, or a celebrity attraction diminishes the clarity of choice of those invited. The lack of inducement keeps a level playing field. When we try to induce people to show up through strong selling or the language of enrolling, we are adding subtle pressure that, in a small but important way, blurs the freely taken decision to say yes.

David Bornstein's research describes how real transformation occurs only through choice. It cannot be sold or mandated. This is particularly true with transformation in community. Institutions and systems can mandate change or attendance from employees because they are under a legal contract. If you don't show up, you violate the contract. This leads to a discussion of consequences, which are very popular in a patriarchal control world.

In an authentic community, citizens decide anew every single time whether to show up. Of course it makes a difference if people do not show up, but we keep inviting them again and again. If they do not choose to show up, there are *no* consequences. They are always welcome. As it is with friends and family. This is what makes volunteer work so maddening—you never know who will show up. The freedom of choice without consequences is also its source of power, for when people do freely decide to show up, it means something more.

The Risks of Invitation

The anxiety of invitation is that if we give them a choice, they might not show up. I do not want to face the reality of their absence, caution, reservations, passivity, or indifference. I do not want to have to face the prospect that I or a few of us may be alone in the future we want to pursue.

And I do not want to face the same truth about myself, for my fear that they will not come is the caution I feel myself about showing up, even for the possibility that I am committed to. My fear is that what I long for is not possible, that what I invite them to is not realistic, that the world I seek cannot exist. And so I imagine myself as a misplaced person, an exile. It is today's version of an old story that I am wrong and I will soon be found out. The fear that no one will show up is a projection of my own doubt, my loss of faith.

Even when we have the power to mandate attendance, the anxiety is that when I instruct them to show up, they may not support the intentions or vision that gave rise to the invitation. The patriarchal fear is that without restraints, incentives, and the use of acceptable force, nothing will get done. The argument for patriarchy is that there are tasks, in which choice—another term for engaging the whole person—is not required or will not contribute to accomplishing the task. This may be true, but the limitation of this stance is that tomorrow may be a little better, but the future will be very much like the past.

The Radical Aspect of Invitation

If the essence of community is to create structures for belonging, then we are constantly inviting people who are strangers to us, and one another, into the circle. An invitation is the antidote to our projection onto those we think are the problem. We take back our projection by extending ourselves to strangers. We make the invitation, in the face of our own isolation, having been waiting to be invited, wanting others to take the first step, wanting others to reach out to us, to acknowledge us and give us the gold star that never came at the right moment. This will never happen, so we are obligated to take the first step.

Invitation may seem simple and straightforward, but it is not. Especially for introverts like me. I have never attended a party without wondering if I had the right night, and have never given a party without believing no one would come.

My friend Ken Murphy and I wanted to convene a Humanities Series for people working in Human Resources (HR) at Philip Morris, where Ken worked at the time. The intent of the series was unusual. It was to imagine a new possibility for HR and do it by bringing people in from outside the field. We selected our faculty: a poet, a philosopher, a theater director, an improvisation actor, a nun, and a city manager. Not your typical faculty for a workshop inside a rather traditional, high-control system.

Our belief was that these people would open our thinking and create space for something new. We also agreed that the series was not designed for better performance, for greater efficiency, or to provide new skills. The invitation would declare that we were interested only in new thinking and therefore we were offering nothing practical, nothing that could be applied to the job in the short run. We also planned to state that the relevance of the experience would be in the hands of the participants. We would make no request of the faculty to ensure the relevance of their presentation.

It took us two years to get up the nerve to make this invitation. Now all these people worked for Ken, so if he had just called a typical meeting or training session, they all would have come. What was interesting was that as straightforward as the invitation might seem (they either come or they don't), giving people real choice in the midst of a patriarchal business institution felt like a radical act. For any of us to offer others real choice in something we care about is always a risk.

Genuine invitation changes our relationship with others, for we come to them as an equal. I must be willing to take no for an answer, without resorting to various forms of persuasion. To sell or induce is not operating by invitation. It is using the language of invitation as a subtle form of control.

This rather purist version of invitation is one reason why you cannot judge success by numbers of people or scale. The pressure for scale will distort the integrity of the invitation. What caused Ken and me to finally go ahead with our Humanities Series was deciding that if only five people accepted the invitation, that would be a beginning and worth the effort. As it turned out, we had 50 seats open, and they were taken immediately.

Invitation as a Way of Being

Invitation is not only a step in bringing people together, it is also a fundamental way of being in community. It manifests the willingness to live in a collaborative way. This means that a future can be created without having to force it or sell it or barter for it. When we believe that barter or subtle coercion is necessary, we are operating out of a context of scarcity and self-interest, the core currencies of the economist. Barter or coercion seems necessary when we have little faith in citizens' desire and capacity to operate out of idealism. The choice for idealism or cynicism is a spiritual stance about the nature of human beings. Cynicism gets justified by naming itself "reality."

A commitment to invitation as a core strategy is betting on a world not dependent on barter and incentives. It is a choice for idealism and determines the context within which people show up. For all the agony of a volunteer effort, you are rewarded by being in the room with people who are up to something larger than their immediate self-interest. You are constantly in the room with people who want to be there, even if their numbers are few. The concern we have about the turnout is simply an expression of our own doubts about the possibility that given a free choice, people will choose to create a future distinct from the past.

Invitation is a language act. "I invite you." Period. This is a powerful conversation because at the moment of inviting, hospitality is created in the world.

• • •

There are certain properties of invitation that can make it more than simply a request. In addition to stating the reason for the gathering, an invitation at its best must contain a hurdle or demand if accepted. This is not to be inhospitable, but to make even the act of invitation an example of the interdependence we want to experience.

So, the invitation is a request not only to show up but to engage. It declares, "We want you to come, but if you do, something will be required from you." Too many leadership initiatives or programs are begun with a sales and marketing mindset: How do we seduce people to sign up and feel good about doing things they may not want to do? Real change, however, is a self-inflicted wound. People need to self-enroll in order to experience their freedom and commitment. Let this begin in the decision to attend, knowing there is a price to be paid far beyond the cost of time and perhaps money.

The Invitation List

The first critical question for ourselves is Kathie Dannemiller's classic, "Who do we need in the room for something different to occur in the world?"

The intent is to bring together people across boundaries. Each person who convenes has a network of relationships with people who might have a stake or interest in the possibility. The challenge is to include the "other" in the conversation. We have to let go of our story about the past. This means you keep inviting those who have not been in the conversation. Even if people say no, that act itself is important and counts for something.

This means that we constantly seek people in the room who are not used to being together. In most cases this would bring together people across sectors (business, education, social services, activists) and, more important (though it is rare) across economic and social classes. Hard work to make this happen, but perhaps more important than what occurs in the gathering.

Marvin Weisbord and Sandra Janoff have given a nice structure to this question in their book *Don't Just Do Something, Stand There!* They want a sample of the "whole system" in the room when they convene for change. They want people with

> authority to act—decision makers;
>
> resources, such as contacts, time, or money;
>
> expertise in the issues to be considered;
>
> information about the topic that no others have;
>
> a need to be involved because they will be affected by the outcome and can speak to the consequences.

The decision about whom to invite is an act of leadership that in and of itself carries a message. Many we invite will choose not to come. This recognizes that for every gathering there are going to be people not in the room who are needed. This is forever the case. It still means that whoever shows up are the right people. Eventually those who do show up always have the task of deciding whom to invite next.

Constructing the Invitation

The elements of invitation are the following:

- Declare the possibility of the gathering
- Frame the choice
- Name the hurdle
- Reinforce the request
- Decide on the most personal form possible

Name the Possibility

The invitation is activated by the possibility we are committed to. This becomes the reason for the gathering. The possibility is a declaration of the future that the convener is committed to. We need to work hard on a statement of possibility that both is compelling to others and inspires us.

Example: The Possibility of a Safe Cincinnati

Harriet Kaufman is committed to the possibility of a safe and peaceful Cincinnati. She believes that what is needed is a conversation that treats violence as a public health issue. She has issued a series of invitiations for people to participate in a community conversation and requires that they engage as active citizens and not come to listen to some experts talk. The moment she makes her invitation, she has brought her possibility into the community.

For Harriet Kaufman's possibility of a safe and peaceful community, she keeps inviting all who have a stake in peace. Youth, public safety, faith community, parents, activists, local government, and more are invited—every time. Everyone in her network gets invited every time. Some show up, some don't, some like the conversation, some don't. Some think violence is a problem for the experts to solve, or a youth problem, or a police problem. Harriet sees the violence, and thinks of the possibility of safety and peace. When Harriet enters the room, safety and peace come with her.

Frame the Choice

We need to pay attention to our willingness and comfort in accepting refusal. This is a whole other conversation discussed later, but for now I'll just say that for an invitation to be authentic, refusal has to be perfectly acceptable. The invitation must allow room for a no. If no is not an option, then it is not an invitation. Framing the choice means we need to be clear that we will not initiate consequences for not attending and that we respect someone's decision not to attend. We choose to have faith that there are good reasons for others not attending what is important to us. Let them know that even if they say no now, they will always be welcome in the future.

Name the Hurdle

We need to tell people explicitly what is required of them should they choose to attend. There is a price to pay for their decision to attend. They will be asked to explore ways to deepen their learning and commitment. Some other common hurdles that should be part of the invitation are: plan to engage with "others," put your interests aside for the moment, commit to the time, and be willing to postpone quick action.

For one series of conversations across boundaries that we held in one section of Cincinnati, we asked people to postpone problem solving and the negotiation of interests. They were not asked to compromise their interests or their constituents' interests, just to hold them to the side for the time being. Here is what the invitation looked like:

1. We come together to create a new possibility through having a conversation we have not had before. We do not come together to negotiate interests, share our stories, or problem-solve the past or future.

2. No one will be asked in any way to yield on their commitments or interests. We are not coming to decide anything. We begin with the belief that the commitments and interests of each of us have to be honored and taken into account by all.

3. Each agrees to participate in all three two-hour discussions. There are always emergencies, and always pressing priorities, but the loss of even one person, for just one meeting, immensely reduces our chance of success.

The most important point is that they were told they would be asked to talk at length, and hopefully strengthen their relationships, with people they have a "story" about.

Paradoxically, even though there is no cost for refusal, there is a price for coming. Everything that has value has a price. Make the purchase price explicit, so that the act of showing up carries some accountability.

Naming the hurdle in the invitation gives us traction in the meeting. When people start to complain, sit in the back of the room, act as if they do not want to be here, and do all the small but noticeable things that hold the action back, we can stand on the fact that they knew what the deal was and still showed up. This gives us the right to ask them what they are doing here. It gives us traction in moving people past their typical story. When they give their habitual explanation about who else needs to change, we can deal with this in a new way, simply because the agreement as to what would be required of them was clear.

The best invitation I have run across, which got a lot of attention for a while, was from Ernest Shackleton, who in the early 1900s was recruiting for an antarctic expedition. Supposedly he ran an ad in the London *Times* that read: "Wanted: Men for Antarctic Expedition. Low Pay. Lousy Food. Safe Return Doubtful." Perfect. He reportedly got 5,000 applicants.

Reinforce the Request

End the invitation by telling people that you want them to come, and that if they choose not to attend, they will be missed but not forgotten.

Make It Personal

In an electronic, need-for-speed, overnight-delivery age, the more personal the invitation the better. A visit is more personal than a call; a call is more personal than a letter; a letter is more personal than e-mail—a letter with six people's names on it is less personal than one addressed to one person, and an e-mail is about as impersonal as it gets. We are so flooded with e-mails and the medium is so senseless that I have come to believe that in the rank order of inviting, e-mails don't count. But all are better than lying in bed at night waiting for the universe to provide.

CHAPTER 12

The Possibility, Ownership, Dissent, Commitment, and Gifts Conversations

After the invitation, there are five other conversations for structuring belonging: possibility, ownership, dissent, commitment, and gifts. Since all the conversations lead to each other, sequence is not that critical. The context of the gathering will often determine which questions to deal with and at what depth. It's important to understand, though, that some are more difficult than others, especially in communities where citizens are just beginning to engage with one another. I present them in ascending order of difficulty, with possibility generally an early conversation to have and gifts typically one of the more difficult.

We are using possibility here in a unique way. Possibility is not a goal or prediction, it is the statement of a future condition that is beyond reach. It works on us and evolves from a discussion of personal crossroads. It is an act of imagination of what we can create together, and it takes the form of a declaration, best made publicly.

The ownership conversation asks citizens to act as if they were creating what exists in the world. Confession is the religious and judicial version of ownership. The distinction is between ownership and blame. The questions for ownership are: "How valuable do you plan for this gathering to be, how have we each contributed to the current situation, and what is the story you hold about this community and your place in it?" It is important for people to see the limitation of their story, for each story has a payoff and a cost. Naming these is a precondition to creating an alternative future.

The dissent conversation creates an opening for commitment. The questions explicitly ask for doubts and reservations. When they are expressed, we need to just listen. Don't solve them, defend against them, or explain anything. People's doubts, cynicism, resignation are theirs alone. Not to be taken on by us. Dissent is distinct from denial, rebellion, and resignation. The questions for dissent are about doubts, refusal, retracting commitments we no longer want to fulfill, owning our lack of forgiveness, and naming our unexpressed resentments.

The commitment conversation is a promise with no expectation of return. Virtue is its own reward. Commitment is distinguished from barter. The enemy of commitment is lip service, not opposition. The commitments that count the most are ones made to peers, other citizens. Not ones made to or by leaders. The questions are variations of "What is the promise I am willing to make?" We have to create space for citizens to declare there is no promise they are willing to make at this time. Refusal to promise does not cost us our membership or seat at the table. We only lose our seat when we do not honor our word.

The most radical and uncomfortable conversation is about our gifts. The leadership and citizen task is to bring the gifts of those on the margin into the center. The gifts conversation is the essence of valuing diversity and inclusion. We are not defined by deficiencies or what is missing. We are defined by our gifts and what is present. This is so for individuals and communities. Belonging occurs when we tell others what gift we receive from them, especially in this moment. When this occurs, in the presence of others, community is built. We embrace our own destiny when we have the courage to acknowledge our own gifts and choose to bring them into the world. The questions for the gift conversations are: "What is the gift you still hold in exile, what is it about you that no one knows, what gratitude has gone unexpressed, and what have others in this room done that has touched you?"

• • •

Conversation Two: Possibility

The possibility conversation frees us to be pulled by a new future. The distinction is between a possibility, which lives into the future, and problem solving, which makes improvements on the past. This distinction takes its value from an understanding that living systems are propelled by the force of the future, and *possibility* as we use it here (thank you, Werner) is one way of speaking of the future.

Possibility occurs as a declaration, and declaring a possibility wholeheartedly can, in fact, be the transformation. The leadership task is to postpone problem solving and stay focused on possibility until it is spoken with resonance and passion. The good news is that once we have fully declared a possibility, it works on us—we do not have to work on it.

The Distinctions for the Possibility Conversation

The challenge with possibility is it gets confused with goals, prediction, and optimism. Possibility is not about what we plan to happen, or what we think will happen, or whether things will get better. Goals, prediction, and optimism don't create anything; they just might make things a little better and cheer us up in the process. Nor is possibility simply a dream. Dreaming leaves us bystanders or observers of our lives. Possibility creates something new. It is a declaration of a future that has the quality of being and aliveness that we choose to live into. It is framed as a declaration of the world that I want to inhabit. It is a statement of who I am that transcends our history, our story, our usual demographics. The power is in the act of declaring.

The distinction between possibility and problem solving is worth dwelling on for a moment. As I have said, surely too many times, we traditionally start with problem solving and talk about goals, targets, resources, and how to persuade others. Even the creation of a vision is part of the problem-solving mentality. A vision is something we must wait for to realize and is most often followed by an effort to make it concrete and practical. Even a vision, which is a more imaginative form of problem solving, needs to be postponed and replaced with possibility. The future is created through a declaration of what is the possibility we stand for. Out of this declaration, each time we enter a room, the possibility enters with us.

The communal possibility comes into being through individual public declarations of possibility. Much the same as witnessing in religious gatherings. Though every possibility begins as an individual declaration, it gains power and impacts community when made public. The community possibility is not the aggregation of individual possibilities. Nor is it a negotiation or agreement on common possibility. The communal possibility is that space or porous container where a collective exists for the realization of all the possibilities of its members. This is the real meaning of a restorative community. It is that place where all possibilities can come alive, and they come alive at the moment they are announced.

• • •

The possibility conversation gives form to one way the gifts of those in the margin get brought into the center. Each person's possibility counts, especially those whose voices are quieted or marginalized by the drumbeat of retribution. In fact, what distinguishes those on the margin in communities is they tragically live without real possibility. For many youth on the margin, the future is narrow, perhaps death or prison. They have trouble imagining a future distinct from the past or present. This is the real tragedy: not only that life is difficult, but that it is a life that holds no possibility for a different future.

Just to be clear about the whole process, the possibility conversation alone does not restore community. The other conversations are just as critical. We have to act as owners of our community, there has to be space for dissent, a commitment has to be made, and gifts have to be embraced. Each conversation takes its life and impact from the other conversations. Even though each leads to the others, any one of them held in isolation reduces the chance of real transformation.

The Questions for the Possibility Conversation

There needs to be a point in each gathering where time is created for the private possibility to be developed and then made public. This works best in two separate steps. The best opening question for possibility is

What is the crossroads where you find yourself at this stage of your life or work or in the project around which we are assembled?

Later, the more direct individual question for possibility will be

What declaration of possibility can you make that has the power to transform the community and inspire you?

There are two overarching questions that point to the future but cannot be asked directly:

What do we want to create together that would make the difference?

What can we create together that we cannot create alone?

These two questions almost define community, for community is that place where these questions are valued. The challenge is that I have never seen them answered in a meaningful way when asked within a context of isolation and disengagement. When people who do not really know each other gather, they are incapable of answering the questions in this most direct and purposeful form. That is why we need the other conversations.

Conversation Three: Ownership

Accountability is the willingness to acknowledge that we have participated in creating, through commission or omission, the conditions that we wish to see changed. Without this capacity to see ourselves as cause, our efforts become either coercive or wishfully dependent on the transformation of others.

Community will be created the moment we decide to act as creators of what it can become. This is the stance of ownership, which is available to us every moment on every issue, even world peace, the overdependence on fossil fuel consumption, and the fact that our teenagers are slightly self-centered.

This requires us to believe in the possibility that this organization, this neighborhood, this community is mine or ours to create. This will occur when we are willing to answer the essential question, "How have I contributed to creating the current reality?" Confusion, blame, and waiting for someone else to change are defenses against ownership and personal power. This core question, when answered, is central to how the community is transformed.

A subtle denial of ownership is innocence and indifference. The future is denied with the response, "It doesn't matter to me—whatever you want to do is fine." This is always a lie and just a polite way of avoiding a difficult conversation around ownership.

People best create that which they own, and cocreation is the bedrock of accountability. The ownership conversation most directly deals with the belief that each of us, perhaps even from the moment of birth, is cause, not effect. The leadership task is to find a way to use this conversation to confront people with their freedom.

The Distinctions for the Conversation for Ownership

Ownership is the decision to become the author of our own experience. It is the choice to decide on our own what value and meaning will occur when we show up. It is the stance that each of us is creating the world, even the one we have inherited.

The key distinction for the conversation is between ownership and blame (a form of entitlement).

We have to realize that each time people enter a room, they walk in with ambivalence, wondering whether this is the right place to be. This is because their default mindset is that someone else owns the room, the meeting, and the purpose that convened the meeting.

Every conventional gathering begins with the unspoken belief that whoever called the meeting has something in mind for us. We are inundated with the world trying to sell us something, so much so that we cannot imagine that this time will be different. This is why so much talk is about others not in the room.

The leader/convener has to act to change this, in a sense to renegotiate the social contract. We want to shift to the belief that this world, including this gathering, is ours to construct together. The intent is to move the social contract from parenting to partnership. Renegotiating the social contract for this room is a metaphoric example of how our social contract with the community can also be renegotiated.

The Questions for Ownership

The idea that "I am cause" can be a difficult question to take on immediately, so lower-risk questions precede a direct approach on this one. The best opening questions are those about the ownership that people feel for this particular gathering. The extent to which they act as owners of this meeting is symptomatic of how they will act as owners of the larger question on the table. The extent of our ownership for larger questions is more difficult and therefore requires a level of relatedness before it can be held in the right context.

Here is a series of questions that have the capacity to shift the ownership of the room.

Four Early Questions

The most effective way to renegotiate the social contract is to ask people to rate on a seven-point scale, from low to high, their responses to four questions:

> **How valuable an experience (or project, or community) do you plan for this to be?**
>
> **How much risk are you willing to take?**
>
> **How participative do you plan to be?**
>
> **To what extent are you invested in the well-being of the whole?**

These are the four questions to ask early in any gathering. People answer them individually, then share their answers in a small group. As mentioned above, be sure to remind them not to give advice, be helpful, or cheer anyone up. Just get interested in whatever the answers are.

The Guilt Question

At some later point, the essential question upon which accountability hinges needs to be asked:

> **What have I done to contribute to the very thing I complain about or want to change?**

This question, higher risk than most others, requires a great deal of trust. It can be asked only after people are connected to each other. This may be the most transforming question of all. If I do not see my part in causing the past and the present, then there is no possible way I can participate usefully in being a coauthor of the future.

Another ownership conversation is to confront our stories, the stories we talked of earlier that limit the possibility of an alternative future. Werner Erhard is so brilliantly clear and creative about this issue.

The sequence he has put together, which I have adapted, goes like this:

What is the story about this community or organization that you hear yourself most often telling? The one that you are wedded to and maybe even take your identity from?

Then ask:

What are the payoffs you receive from holding on to this story?

The payoffs are usually in the neighborhood of being right, being in control, being safe. Or not being wrong, controlled, or at risk.

And finally:

What is your attachment to this story costing you?

The cost, most often, is our sense of aliveness.

These are the questions that allow us to complete our stories. Not forget them, but complete them. The naming of the story to another, in the context we have created, can take the limiting power out of the story. This allows the story to stay in the past and creates an opening for us to move forward.

A friendly warning: Don't ever underestimate the determination of people to hold on to their stories, no matter the cost or the suffering they sustain. Most of us are not willing to give up our story in the moment, but this process works on us over time.

Conversation Four: Dissent

Creating space for dissent is the way diversity gets valued in the world. Inviting dissent into the conversation is how we show respect for a wide range of beliefs. It honors the Bohr maxim that for every great idea, the opposite idea is also true.

There is no way to be awake in the world without having serious doubts and reservations. Each of us takes many walks in the desert, and in some ways our faith is measured by the extent of our doubts. Without doubt, our faith has no meaning, no substance; it is purchased at too small a price to give it value.

This sounds simple and true enough, but in a patriarchal world, dissent is considered disloyalty. Or negativism. Or not being a team player. Or not being a good citizen. America, love it or leave it. You are either with us or against us. This is a corruption of hospitality and friendship. Hospitality is the welcoming not only of strangers, but also of the strange ideas and beliefs they bring with them.

Doubt and Dissent

A critical task of leadership is to protect space for the expression of people's doubts. The act of surfacing doubts and dissent does not deflect the communal intention to create something new. What is critical, and hard to live with, is that leaders do not have to respond to each person's doubts. None of us do. Authentic dissent is complete simply in its expression. When we think we have to answer people's doubts and defend ourselves, then the space for dissent closes down. When people have doubts, and we attempt to answer them, we are colluding with their reluctance to be accountable for their own future. All we have to do with the doubts of others is get interested in them. We do not have to take them on or let them resonate with our own doubts. We just get interested.

One place where this is least understood is in the relationship between police and citizens. Few civil servants put themselves at such risk or are more vulnerable than the police. No civil servants are literally more physically present in a community than police. Police are constantly in community conversations talking about public safety.

Police get into a problem when they think they are *responsible* for public safety. They are not. Citizens are responsible for public safety; citizens commit crimes, prevent crimes, and create the conditions where crime is high or low. As long as police take responsibility for safety, they are going to stay in a defensive stance, which moves nothing forward. Police are responsible for enforcing the law, apprehending criminals, and mediating or stopping violence. Police are not suppliers of safety to a passive citizenry. Safety is not a product purchased from the police. When citizens want to place responsibility for safety on the police, and police defend themselves, they collude with citizen unwillingness to claim their sidewalks and community as their own.

Listening is the action step that replaces defending ourselves. Listening, understanding at a deeper level than is being expressed, is the action that creates a restorative community. This does not mean that police, in this case, do not need to change or be involved in later problem solving; of course they do, as do the rest of us. It does mean that instead of answering every question, defending their actions, they can ask questions to find out more about the concerns, the doubts, and even the lives of citizens. No one understands this more than Mike Butler, police chief of Longmont, Colorado. One of Mike's favorite statements is: "For 80 percent of the calls we receive, people do not need a uniformed officer, they need a neighbor." Wise man.

This then is a key role of leadership: get interested in people's dissent, their doubts, and find out why this matters so much to them. Dissent becomes commitment and accountability when we get interested in it without having to fix, explain, or answer it. Granted, sometimes other things masquerade as authentic dissent, which will be discussed a little later.

No Is the Beginning of Commitment

The dissent conversation begins by allowing people the space to say no. It rests on the belief that if we cannot say no, then our yes has no meaning.

Each of us needs the chance to express our doubts and reservations, without having to justify them or to move quickly into problem solving. "No" is the beginning of the conversation for commitment. This is critical: that dissent is followed by the other conversations. To create space for dissent is not to leave it hanging there, but to move on to the other conversations of possibility, ownership, and gifts.

The fear is that we will make people more negative by making room for refusal. The mental model of the ostrich. If people say no, it does not create their dissent, it only expresses it. It also does not mean they will get their way. Restorative community is that place where saying no doesn't cost us our membership in the meeting or in the community. Encourage those who say no to stay—we need their voice.

We will let go of only those doubts that we have given voice to. When someone authentically says no, then the room becomes real and trustworthy. An authentic statement is one in which the person owns that the dissent is their choice and not a form of blame or complaint. The power in the expression of doubts is that it gives us choice about them. Once expressed, they no longer control us; we control them.

Doubt and "no" are symbolic expressions of people finding their space and role in the future. It is when we fully understand what people do not want that choice becomes possible. Dissent in this way is life giving, or life affirming. It is the refusal to live the life someone else has in mind for us. As an individual, it is the moment when we acknowledge that we are not the children our parents, guardians, teachers had in mind. We have disappointed others and for too long internalized that disappointment. The moment we say no to the expectations of others about who they wish us to be, the moment we declare, "I am not that person," our adulthood begins. Just because it took 30 or 40 years, this is no time to get picky.

Same in community. The moment people experience the fact that they can dissent, or, in softer form, express doubts, and not lose their place in the circle, they begin to join as full-fledged citizens. When dissent is truly valued and becomes the object of genuine curiosity, the chance of showing up as an owner of that circle, that room, that neighborhood goes up dramatically.

Distinctions for the Conversation for Dissent

There is a vital difference between authentic dissent and inauthentic dissent, which we can call false refusal. Inauthentic forms of dissent are denial, rebellion, and resignation.

Denial means we act as if the present is good enough. It is defense against the woundedness of the present and a rejection of any possibility beyond continuous improvement. Our denial of the destruction of the environment is a good example. Denial in this case takes the form of wanting more data or holding the belief that technology is a god that can surmount any obstacle. It often agrees there is a problem, but then trivializes its existence or its cost.

Denial is a defining feature of addiction. In creating the communities we live in, we are addicted to urban centers and rural towns that don't work for all, to a world of large class differences, to a place where we consider people on the margin to not be our brothers and sisters. We are addicted to accepting the illusion of safety that we get from allowing large systems to name the game and define the conversation.

Rebellion is more complex. It lives in reaction to the world. On the surface, rebellion claims to be against monarchy, dominion, or oppression. Too often it turns out to be a vote *for* monarchy, dominion, or patriarchy. Rebellion is most often not a call for transformation or a new context, but simply a complaint that others control the monarchy and not us. This is why most revolutions fail—because nothing changes, only the name of the monarch.

The community form of rebellion is protest. It is noble in tradition but still often keeps us in perpetual reaction to the stances of others. There is safety in building an identity on what we do not want. The extremists on both sides of any issue are more wedded to their positions than to creating a new possibility. That is why they make unfulfillable demands. The AM radio band is populated with this non-conversation. Any time we act in reaction, even to evil, we are giving power to what we are in reaction to.

I have heard John McKnight say that advisory groups speak quietly to power, protestors scream at power, and neither chooses to reclaim or produce power. The real problem with rebellion is that it is such fun. It avoids taking responsibility, operates on the high ground, is fueled by righteousness, gives legitimacy to blame, and is a delightful escape from the unbearable burden of being accountable. It has much to recommend it.

Resignation is the ultimate act of powerlessness and a stance against possibility. It is a passive form of control. It is born of our cynicism and loss of faith. What we are resigning from is the future and what we are embracing is the past. None of us is strong enough to carry the dead weight of others' resignation or even our own. Resignation ultimately alienates us and destroys community. It is the spiritual cause of isolation and not belonging. Beware of resignation, for it presents itself as if data and experience were on its side.

Dissent, as a form of refusal, becomes authentic when it is a choice for its own sake. When it is an act of accountability. Authentic dissent is recognizable by the absence of blame, the absence of resignation. Blame, denial, rebellion, and resignation have no power to create. A simple *no* begins a larger conversation, or at least creates the space for one.

We help this when we realize there is nothing to argue about. Once again, when faced with a no, or doubts, or authentic refusal, we move forward when we get interested and curious.

The Questions for Dissent

The challenge is to frame the questions in a way that evokes dissent that is authentic. We do not want to encourage, through our selection of questions, any kind of denial, rebellion, or resignation. To circumvent denial, don't ask people whether they think there is a problem. Or even ask them to define the problem. Do not ask people what they are going to do, or to list the ten characteristics of anything. The way to avoid rebellion is to stop trying to sell or control the world. When faced with rebellion, all we can do is recognize it, not argue.

Some questions for the expression of dissent:

What doubts and reservations do you have?

What is the no, or refusal, that you keep postponing?

What have you said yes to, that you no longer really mean?

What is a commitment or decision that you have changed your mind about?

What forgiveness are you withholding?

What resentment do you hold that no one knows about?

These are in ascending order of difficulty. The final two are very difficult and should be used with discretion. I always offer them as a possible conversation, for I know that if people do not want to answer a question, they won't and no damage is done. We can ask anything, as long as we do not pressure people in any way to answer.

The key for the leader/convener is not to take the dissent personally or to argue in any way with the doubts that get expressed. If you can genuinely answer a question that resolves the doubt, then do so. Most of the time, however, the doubts are well founded and have no easy answer, so all we can do is appreciate that the doubt was made public.

The intent is for concerns to be expressed openly, not left to quiet conversations in the hallways, among allies, or in the restrooms. Dissent is a form of caring, not one of resistance.

Conversation Five: Commitment

Commitment usually comes later in the process, after the first four conversations and some of the work on substantive issues has been done.

Commitment is a promise made with no expectation of return. It is the willingness to make a promise independent of either approval or reciprocity from other people. This takes barter out of the conversation. Our promise is not contingent on the actions of others. The economist is replaced by the artist. As long as our promise is dependent on the actions of others, it is not a commitment; it is a deal, a contract. A bargained future is not an alternative future; it is more of the past brought forward.

The declaration of a promise is the form that commitment takes; that is the action that initiates change. It is one thing to set a goal or objective, but something more personal to use the language of promises. Plus, to the extent that a promise is a sacred form of expression, this language anoints the space in the asking.

Lip Service Is the Enemy of Commitment

Sometimes we act as if we need to choose between commitment and refusal or dissent. They are friendly to each other, and both important conversations. Saying no is a stance as useful as a promise. Both offer clarity and the authentic basis to move forward, even if there is no place to go at the moment. Lip service is another story. Nothing kills democracy or transformation faster than lip service. The future does not die from opposition; it disappears in the face of lip service.

The key distinction is between commitment and barter, but what is most dangerous to commitment is lip service. Lip service sabotages commitment. It offers an empty step forward. It comes in the form of "I'll try." It is an agreement made standing next to the exit door. Whenever someone says they will try hard, agree to think about it, or do the best they can, it is smart to consider that a no. It may not be a final refusal, but at that moment there is no commitment. We can move forward with refusal; we cannot move forward with maybe. Trying hard is too often a coded refusal. Whether it is a response to feeling coerced, a sense of internal obligation, or just a desire to look good, it is really a way to escape the moment and hijacks commitment.

Wholehearted commitment makes a promise to peers about our contribution to the success of the whole. It is centered in two questions: "What promise am I willing to make?" and "What is the price I am willing to pay for the success of the whole effort?" It is a promise for the sake of a larger purpose, not for the sake of personal return. Commitment comes dressed as a promise.

Another key is to see the importance of the words "a promise to peers." More on this below, but peers receive the promises and determine whether the promises are enough to bring an alternative future into existence. The convener's task is to direct the eyes and words of citizens toward each other. That is why we have people sit in circles, facing one another.

What reassures in this process is that we need the commitment of much fewer people than we thought to create the future we have in mind.

The Questions for the Conversation for Commitment

Commitment embraces two kinds of promises:

- My behavior and actions with others
- Results and outcomes that occur in the world

As suggested above, promises that matter are those made to peers, not those made to people who have power over us (parents, bosses, leaders). The future is created through the exchange of promises between citizens, the people with whom we have to live out the intentions of the change. It is to these people that we give our commitments, and it is they who decide if our offer is enough—for the person, for the institution, for the community. Peers have the right to declare that the promise made is not enough to serve the interests of the whole. As in each act of refusal, this is the beginning of a longer conversation.

Promises are sacred. They are the means by which we choose accountability. We become accountable the moment we make them public.

Depending on our taste and intuition, here is a menu of questions for this conversation:

What promises am I willing to make?

What measures have meaning to me?

What price am I willing to pay?

What is the cost to others for me to keep my commitments, or to fail in my commitments?

What is the promise I'm willing to make that constitutes a risk or major shift for me?

What is the promise I am postponing?

What is the promise or commitment I am unwilling to make?

If you really want to ground this conversation, write the promises by hand, and sign and date them. Then collect and publish the whole set. About once a quarter, meet and ask, "How's it going?"

A note: "I am willing to make no promise at this moment" is a fine and acceptable stance. It is a commitment of another kind. Saying "I pass" is an act of citizen refusal that is ennobling. This means that refusal does not cost someone their membership in the circle. We need to hold the space for that kind of refusal. When we honor the refusal of one person, we honor that choice for all persons. When one person says no, that person is speaking in some way for all of us. Holding space for refusal in the midst of a conversation for commitment gives depth and substance to the choice or commitment all others have made.

The only act that puts membership at risk is the unwillingness to honor our word. This is the choice to not fulfill our promises or not retract them when we know they will not be fulfilled. Refusing to make a promise is an act of integrity and supports community. Not being a person who honors our word by either fulfilling our promises or retracting when we know they will not be fulfilled sabotages community, and it does not matter what the excuse.

Conversation Six: Gifts

In our attraction to problems, deficiencies, disabilities, and needs, the missing community conversation is about gifts. The only cultural practices that focus on gifts are retirement parties and funerals. We only express gratitude for your gifts when you are on your way out or gone. If we really want to know what gifts others see in us, we have to wait for our own eulogy, and even then, as the story goes, we will miss it by a few days.

In community building, rather than focusing on our deficiencies and weaknesses, which will most likely not go away, we gain more leverage when we focus on the gifts we bring and seek ways to capitalize on them. Instead of problematizing people and work, the conversation that searches for the mystery of our gifts brings the greatest change and results.

The focus on gifts confronts people with their essential core, that which has the potential to make the difference and change lives for good. This resolves the unnatural separation between work and life. Who we are at work is our life. Who we are in life is our work. The leadership task—indeed the task of every citizen—is to bring the gifts of those on the margin into the center. This applies to each of us as an individual, for our life work is to bring our gifts into the world. This is a core quality of a hospitable community, whose work is to bring into play the gifts of all its members, especially strangers.

The Gifts Distinctions

Authentic acknowledgment of our gifts is what it means to be inclusive or to value diversity. Judith Snow, a powerful voice in the so-called disabilities world, declares that the purpose of her life is to eliminate the language of disabilities from our vocabulary. She stated in an e-mail to me, "My deepest desire is to make the world safe for people whose abilities and contributions are generally unrecognized." She creates a world where no one is known, is labeled, or takes their identity from their disabilities, only from their gifts. This is in no way a denial of our limitations, just a recognition that they are not who we are. I am not what I am not able to do. I am what I am able to do—my gifts and capacities.

The point is that an alternative future occurs when we capitalize on our gifts and capacities. Bringing the gifts of those on the margin into the center is a primary task of leadership and citizenship.

The distinction here is straightforward, between gifts and deficiencies.

When we look at deficiencies, we strengthen them. What you see is what you get. When you label or name me arrogant or quietly aggressive, which I am, that is what you are going to get. In this way, the focus on gifts is a practical stance, not a moral one. What do you want from me—my deficiencies or my capacities?

The Questions for the Conversation of Gifts

The gifts conversation boils down to our willingness to stop telling people about

> what they need to improve
>
> what didn't go well
>
> how they should do it differently next time

Instead, confront them with their gifts. Talk to others about

> the gifts you've received from them
>
> the unique strength that you see in them
>
> the capacities they have that bring something unique and needed in the world
>
> what they did in the last ten minutes that made a difference

Gifts of This Gathering

Every time we gather, there needs to be space for a discussion of what gifts have been exchanged. This question needs to be asked of the community:

What gift have you received from another in this room? Tell the person in specific terms.

We focus on gifts because what we focus on, we strengthen. The gifts-of-this-gathering question can be asked this way:

What has someone in your small group done today that has touched you or moved you or been of value to you?

or

In what way did a particular person engage you in a way that had meaning?

In practical terms, this means that in each small group, one person at a time tells the others what they have received and appreciated from others.

Because we are so awkward about this kind of discussion, the conversation needs to be set up in a special way. We ask the person who hears about what they have given another to say, "Thank you, I like hearing that." We want to let the statements of gifts to have a chance to sink in. Don't deflect the appreciation. Help them put aside the routine of denying their gifts. Encourage them not to say that others brought it out of them, or what a great group this is, or how they got lucky for once and will try to not let it happen again.

This means we enforce a complete ban on denying gifts and discussing weaknesses and what is missing. No human problem solving allowed. Often, people, so conditioned by the retributive culture that we have experienced, want negative feedback. This is packaged in the name of learning and growth.

Don't buy the packaging. The longing for feedback that we can "work on" is really a defense against the terrible burden of acknowledging our gifts and getting about the work of living into them, which we can call "fulfilling our destiny"—language so demanding and imposing, no wonder I would rather keep swimming in the morass of my needs and incompleteness.

> Among all the things which God created in His universe, He created nothing that is useless. He created the snail as a cure for a wound, the fly as a cure for the sting of the wasp, the gnat as a cure for the bite of the serpent, the serpent as a cure for a sore, and the spider as a cure for the sting of a scorpion.
>
> Shabbat 77b, Babylonian Talmud, from *Judaism and Social Justice*, by Harriet Kaufman

The Gift Each Brings to the World

Beyond the conversation about what gifts occurred in this gathering, we each have to deal with the extent that we are bringing the gifts given to us at birth or beyond into the world. We are aware of our deficiencies beyond belief or utility. What we are blind to are our gifts, the ones unique to us. These are qualities we have not earned but that have come to us as an act of grace. Our work in life is to know and accept these gifts, for this is what is required to bring them forth.

The questions to ask are the following:

What is the gift you currently hold in exile?

What is it about you that no one knows about?

What are you grateful for that has gone unspoken?

What is the positive feedback you receive that still surprises you?

What is the gift you have that you do not fully acknowledge?

As with all the conversations, there may be no immediate and clear answers to these questions. It doesn't matter. The questions themselves work on us, and when they are asked, this work is activated. In the asking, we are creating space for gifts, which are central to restoration, restoration that wants to occur at this moment. The questions, in this way, are the transformation, simply by being named.

The Questions at a Glance

The heart of the conversations emerging from all of these questions is to create a sense of belonging with others and also a sense of accountability for oneself.

Here is a summary of the core questions associated with each conversation:

To what extent are you here by choice? (Invitation)

How much risk do you plan to take and how participative do you plan to be in this gathering or project? (Ownership)

What are the crossroads you/we are at appropriate to the purpose of the gathering? (Possibilities)

What declarations are you prepared to make about the possibilities for the future? (Possibilities)

To what extent do you see yourself as cause of the problem you are trying to fix? (Ownership)

What is the story you hold about this community or this issue, and what are the payoffs and cost of this story? (Ownership)

What are your doubts and reservations? (Dissent)

What is the yes you no longer mean? (Dissent)

What promises are you willing to make to your peers? (Commitment)

What gifts have you received from each other? (Gifts)

The important thing about these questions is that they name the agenda that can shift the nature of the future. They are a curriculum for restorative community. The power is in the asking, not in the answers. And we do not have to get it just right. There are many ways to frame the questions, as long as we do not make the way too easy. The work is to invent questions that fit the business you are up to and the conditions you are attempting to shift.

> When a child is born, they are bringing a gift from the spirit world that the community needs.
>
> Sobonfu

A final caveat. These ideas and methodology depend on a certain amount of good will. When individuals or communities are more committed to being right than to creating an alternative future, then nothing we do can make much of a difference. There are those times and places where the cynicism, despair, and resignation run so deep that all that we attempt seems to fall on deaf ears. In the long run, I do not believe this is ever the case. But there are moments, specific gatherings, that just do not go well. At these times, all we can do is forgive ourselves for how little difference we seem to have made and then perhaps have a conversation with God.

Bringing Hospitality
into the World

We usually associate hospitality with a culture, a social practice, a more personal quality to be admired. In western culture, where individualism and security seem to be priorities, we need to be more thoughtful about how to bring the welcoming of strangers into our daily way of being together.

•   •   •

The six conversations have power when they occur in a context of hospitality. Here are the design elements for structuring hospitality into our gatherings.

Welcome and Greeting

Greet people at the door; welcome them personally and help them get seated. People enter in isolation. Reduce the isolation they came with; let them know they came to the right place and are not alone.

Example: Carlsbad, California

When Ray Patchett, city manager of Carlsbad, California, decided to involve the community in determining its future, he and his staff placed a red carpet from the street to the front door of the meeting place. They had people at the door to welcome people and escort them to the meeting room. At the meeting room, each citizen was personally introduced to other citizens. A local group was playing music, light food was offered. Photos taken by children were on the wall. Get the picture? When you came to this meeting, you knew you had come to the right place. Of course this took some time and effort on the part of the city manager team, but what a message of care and inclusion for the citizens of Carlsbad.

Restate the Invitation

After the welcome, begin with a statement of why you are there. Declare the possibility that led to the invitation. Use everyday language and speak from the heart, without PowerPoint presentations, slides, video, and so on. Use words and phrases that express choice, optimism, faith, willingness to act, commitment to persevere, and the fact that the leaders came to listen, not just to speak.

Connection Before Content

Before diving into the agenda, citizens need to be connected to one another. Whenever we enter a room, it is with doubt and a vague feeling of isolation. Connecting citizens to each other is not intended to be just an icebreaker, which is fun yet does little to break the isolation or create community. Icebreakers will achieve contact but not connection. Connection occurs when we speak of what matters about this moment. This is done most easily through questions (surprise!).

Some examples of connection questions:

What led you to accept the invitation?

What would it take for you to be fully present in this room?

What is the price others paid for you to be here?

If you could invite someone you respect to sit beside you and support you in making this meeting successful, whom would that be?

Since connection occurs most easily in small face-to-face groupings, create circles of three or six. Request that people to sit with those they know the least—it gives each person the freedom to be who they are and not whom their colleagues think they should be. It also symbolizes the intent to have people move beyond the boundaries of their own history and alliance.

Certain groupings are better for learning and connection; others are better for closure and problem solving. Use a diverse mix of people, people who know each other the least, early in the gathering. This "maximum mix" is good for opening questions and raising doubts. Use affinity groupings, those who are most familiar with each other, for planning actions and making promises.

One structural sequence for creating community is to start with the individuals reflecting on the question, and then have them talk in trios, next in groups of six, and then to the whole community. Shorthand is 1-3-6-all.

Late Arrivals

Someone always comes late, especially in community work. This does not mean we do not start on time, but the fact that a person showed up needs to be acknowledged. Welcome them without humiliation and connect them to the group. Restored community is created when every gathering is a demonstration of the future we came to create, so we need to take a moment to include those who come late. This is a defining feature of a culture of hospitality, and often taking the time to welcome a latecomer sets the tone for what we consider to be important, which is relatedness.

Early Departure

When a participant leaves early, there is a hole and a kind of emptiness left behind. The early exit leaves a void in the community. It hurts the community; there is a cost, a consequence to the community. This takes energy and resources from the gathering and is unavoidably wounding to the experience of community and belonging.

Take this seriously. Loss is an element of engagement. Treat the loss of a member as important as the welcome and the conclusion of the gathering. Here is a way to handle early departures that reflects that spirit:

Ask in the beginning for people to give notice of leaving. Ask them to leave in public, not to sneak out in the dark of night or in silence or during a break.

Acknowledge their leaving in a deliberate way.

Have them announce to the group that they are leaving and where they are going. This will create some discomfort, but that is the nature of separation.

Have three people from the group say, "Here's what you've given us . . ." This is a moment for the gifts conversation.

Ask the soon-to-be-departed, "What are you taking with you? What shifted for you, became clearer? What value have you received as a result of being here? Is there anything else you'd like to say to the community?"

Thank them for coming.

Remove their chairs—if the chairs remain empty, it only reminds us of our loss.

All of this takes time, but we are choosing depth over speed. Plus, how we treat that person today is how we will be treated tomorrow.

Breaking Bread Together

In creating the conversation and social space that support community, another dimension of welcome is what has traditionally defined culture: food. It brings the sacred into the room. It is the symbol of hospitality. It is as direct as we can be about a life-giving act. When we take it seriously, we know how to do this right. What is needed is consciousness about having food and what kind of food fits our intention.

One small request: Most food served in meetings is about satiation, not about health. Even in health care settings or meetings about creating healthy communities, we serve pastries, cookies, fast food, chips, pretzels. This is not food; it is fuel and habit that is nutritionally and environmentally unconscious.

Let there be apples so that we have some way of moving beyond the illusion of paradise; grapes for the sake of pleasure; bread, unleavened if you can find it, a reminder of the Sabbath . . . you get the point. Natural, healthy food, prepared by local merchants. Food that reflects the diversity of the world we are embracing. Grown within 50 miles of our gathering place to reduce the carbon footprint.

Some people will complain. Let them.

CHAPTER 14

Designing Physical Space
That Supports Community

Physical space is more decisive in creating community than
we realize. Most meeting spaces are designed for control, negotiation,
and persuasion. While the room itself is not going to change, we always
have a choice about how we rearrange and occupy whatever room
we are handed. Community is built when we sit in circles, when there
are windows and the walls have signs of life, when every voice can be
equally heard and amplified, when we all are on one level—and the
chairs have wheels and swivel.

*When we have an opportunity to design new space, the same
communal consciousness applies. We need reception areas that tell us
we are in the right place and are welcome, hallways wide enough for
intimate seating and casual contact, eating spaces that refresh us and
encourage relatedness, meeting rooms designed with nature, art, conviviality, and citizen-to-citizen interaction in mind. And we need large
community spaces that have those qualities of great communal intimacy.*

*Finally, the design process itself needs to be an example of the future
we are intending to create. The material and built world is a reflection
of the connectedness, openness, and curiosity of the group gathered to
design the space. Authentic citizen engagement is as important as design
expertise.*

• • •

The discussion to this point has been about creating a new
communal conversation by redesigning the social space within

which we gather. There is one more aspect of conversation that is important to creating the experience of community and belonging. This is to be intentional about how we design and occupy physical space.

The Physical Space

The room has importance beyond its functionality. Every room we occupy serves as a metaphor for the larger community that we want to create. This is true socially and also physically. The room is the visible expression of today's version of the future. The room we are in, and how we choose to occupy it, is what we have to work with in the present moment. If the future we desire does not exist in this room, today, then it will never occur tomorrow. This is what is meant by "Change the room, change the culture."

Meeting rooms are traditionally designed for efficiency, control, and business as we know it.

> **Conference rooms** have long rectangular tables basically designed for negotiation, one side facing the other. The effect is that you can only see those on "the other side." You sit blind to those on your own side of the table. Yet here we are, gathering to build community, accountability, and relatedness, and we cannot make eye contact with half the people in the room.
>
> The ends of the table are VIP positions. We all know this and avoid these seats. They are most often occupied last. In a restaurant, the one at the end of the table usually ends up paying the bill, so who wants to sit there by choice? This is also the typical design for boardrooms, which are all about prestige, privilege, and control.
>
> **Auditoriums** are designed for citizens to passively receive what others have produced. They are great for presentation and performance which leaves the audience with their backs turned to each other, all eyes facing front.
>
> **Classrooms** are mostly designed for instruction. The usual layout says there will be one expert who knows, 10 to 300 students who are there to absorb what the expert knows. Structured for teaching, not

learning. This arrangement gives little recognition to the importance of peer-to-peer learning. Sometimes we see the hollow square or U-shaped arrangement of tables and chairs. Same problem: Each person loses sight of one-third to one-quarter of the people in the room, and those we can see are on the other side of a moat of empty space.

Reception areas are mostly designed for security. The message is that you have to demonstrate your right to enter this building. Hardly the welcome that encourages belonging. If you want to see a reception area designed for welcoming and hospitality, visit a nice hotel, a bar, or a good restaurant.

Hallways are designed for transportation. There are a growing number of community-conscious buildings that create hallways as city streets—places where casual contact is valued, the rooms you pass have internal windows like storefronts, and the hallway is wide enough for sitting areas. All created to bring life to our experience.

Cafeterias are often designed as efficient refueling stations. The concern seems to be how many people can we feed and how quickly. Chairs, tables, walls, food stations are set up for efficiency, easy maintenance, don't linger, please get back to work. As if sitting and being with other employees is not work.

Bringing the Room to Life and Life to the Room

While we may not have control over the form and shape of the room, we always have choices about how to occupy the room. The task is to rearrange the room to meet our intention to build relatedness, accountability, and commitment. This puts the convener in the role of interior designer. I spend my life being neurotically fussy about what room to meet in, and how to rearrange it once I get there. This is embarrassing, awkward, gets weird looks, receives irrational refusals, and sometimes you just get tired lugging chairs around the room. But this is work that has to be done in a world not designed for human interaction.

The room needs to express the quality of aliveness and belonging that we wish for the community. Here is what this entails:

Arrange the Room as the Shape of Things to Come

The circle is the geometric symbol for community, and therefore for arranging the room. No tables if possible. If tables are a given, then choose round ones (the shape of communion), which are better than rectangles (the shape of negotiation), or classroom-style tables (the shape of instruction). If tables are a given, find the smallest ones you can.

The ideal seating for a small group is a circle of chairs with no table. Put the chairs as close together as possible, which forces people to lean in to one another.

Pick a Room with a View

A room without windows blocks out the larger world that we are attempting to care for. A room with no windows carries the message that the larger world does not, for this moment, exist. It isolates us from that larger world and gives permission to be focused narrowly on the smaller world within the boundaries of our own interests. It makes the neighborhood, the city, and the globe invisible. It also keeps the energy produced by our gathering trapped in too small a space. There is no exchange of energy between our work and the world when we are trapped in a box.

Welcome Nature into the Room

Gather near a window, if there is one. Open the curtains; pull up the shades or blinds. If there is too much light to see the PowerPoint presentation, so be it. Perhaps there is a message in this.

Bring in plants, even if they are artificial. As my friend Allan Cohen says, artificial plants are real, they are real plastic. The walls and furnishings of most of our meeting places are dead. The spaces are designed in the name of modernity, efficiency, and low maintenance. We do not have to passively acquiesce to this.

Amplify the Whole Room

All voices need to be heard equally, and we have the technology to amplify a whole room. Look at a concert hall if you doubt this.

I met a conservation commissioner in Colorado who was constantly arbitrating disputes between ranchers, farmers, environmentalists, loggers, and all who care about our open spaces. He decided to buy a van and amplification equipment so that wherever in the state he went, he could mike the room. All could speak without walking up to a podium, and all could be heard equally. He said that as soon as he made this investment, the tone of the conversations shifted. The differences did not go away, but the contentiousness of the debate subsided, and civility and respect increased.

Choose Chairs That Swivel and Have Wheels and Low Backs

A chair is not just for support; it is also a means of mobility and transportation. Most meeting room chairs are designed for straight lines and stability. If you place them in circles and move too much, they get nervous and unhappy.

If designed well, a chair can encourage movement from one small group to another. It can facilitate moving our attention back and forth from our small group to the larger forum. A movable chair is a metaphor for the need to move back and forth from the concern for local tribal integrity and the needs of the whole.

A swivel chair tells us that we must keep rotating to take in all that is around us so that what we create in our own unit or neighborhood occurs in the context of a larger world. Wheels allow us to move among small groups easily. If there are wheels on the chair, they ask to be used and serve to convince us that we are at every moment connected and willing to travel to all else that is happening in the room.

Level the Playing Field

Rooms in public buildings, presumably designed for civic dialogue, often have a stage or raised platform. A platform or stage creates a demand for performance and judgment; it looks like the throne of the monarch, the bench of the judge. This is not the arrangement for democracy or community. Granted, watching a stage together gives us a common experience, but it does not connect citizens to each other. When we watch the stage together, we have once again turned our backs on each other. This obliterates the circle, the traditional shape of community.

The raised platform, besides underlining the superiority of a few raised higher than the heads of many others, distorts the need for dialogue by encouraging questions and answers. It's as if citizens can show up only with questions, and the leaders will be the ones with the answers. Question and answer sessions are patriarchy's answer to interaction.

Most city councils operate from raised platforms that isolate elected officials from citizens. Those platforms are effective in establishing the authority of the leaders and good for creating order. They are weak in creating a structure where the leaders themselves are physically structured to work well together. Plus the leader who would declare to citizens that we want your input, and do this while looking down on them—from behind a big table, sitting on a plush chair, speaking into his own microphone—makes the intention impossible to implement. In these situations, the leader is as imprisoned by the structure as the citizen.

Even in the theater, which is traditionally all about performance, there are structures designed to reduce the social and emotional distance between actor and audience. Theaters in the round put the stage in the center of the space so that the audience becomes a participant in the drama.

Bring in Art and the Aesthetic

This is a larger conversation than can be dealt with here, but here is the gist of it. There can be no transformation without art. Art in the form of theater, poetry, music, dance, literature, painting, and sculpture. Communities by and large know this and invest heavily in the arts. Those who want to heal the wounds of a fragmented community initiate hundreds of art projects for those living on the margin. Art brings these voices into the mainstream. Most communities are proud of their arts tradition and rightly so.

If this is true for our larger communities, then it must be present each time we gather.

Why would we assemble without a moment of silence, a song, a recitation? We often have this consciousness in education, workshops, and conferences. This sensibility should not be sequestered into those special occasions but be a part of our daily life. If every gathering is an occasion for producing for ourselves a future we want to inhabit, then we need to design it for that intention and we need art to accomplish this.

If it is a large gathering, invite a local band or choir or dance troupe to welcome people into the session. Each time you break and reconvene, create some form of art or inspiration to mark the transition. Read a poem, or take a moment to create a poem, write in a journal, breathe together. This is all very doable with little cost or preparation.

Every group of 20 people has someone who would be willing to sing a song, recite a poem, or tell a story. All we need to do is make the request at the beginning of the gathering, and as people come to trust each other, someone will offer their gift of song, poem, or story to the community. When this happens, the tone in the room shifts and the place becomes a little more sacred.

Put Life on the Wall

There is nothing as lonely as an empty wall. Our halls and meeting spaces are filled with empty walls. Interestingly, this is not true of executive offices or spaces designed for sales presentations. Great attention is paid to making these places warm and welcoming. Art collections adorn the walls, seating is comfortable, and windows are softened with fabric. Granted, this decoration serves as a sign of privilege and importance, but it is a good thing. Why not extend this symbolism to those spaces where citizens and employees gather?

"An empty wall is a testimony to the insignificance of the human spirit," observed pioneering street life researcher William H. Whyte. Our job is to affirm the significance of the human spirit, and filling the walls with photos and with art by citizens, youth, and employees is very doable. The library or art galleries in the community would be willing to curate public space. They do it frequently for restaurants and shops. It is not a question of cost; it is a question of consciousness.

At the end of the day, we have to ask, how can we create aliveness when the wall sits sadly empty?

Design and Build Opportunities

Every once in a while, there comes an opportunity to work with architects to design new spaces that support community. These are rare moments (unless you are an architect) when we can bring a communal consciousness to the construction of a new building or the rehabilitation of an old one.

An elegant quote from Christopher Alexander in Book One of his *Nature of Order* series reminds us how rare and powerful are these opportunities to bring a new consciousness into the material world:

> Common sense tells us—or seems to tell us—that the physical environment affects our lives. It has often been said, certainly, that the shape of buildings affects our ability to live, our well-being, perhaps our behavior. Winston Churchill is believed to have said, "we shape our buildings; and they shape us." But *how* do they affect us?
>
> I shall argue that the geometry of the physical world—its space—has the most profound impact possible on human beings: it has impact on the most important of all human qualities, our inner freedom, or the sense of life each person has. It touches on internal freedom, freedom of the spirit.
>
> I shall argue that the right kind of physical environment, when it has living structure, nourishes freedom of the spirit in human beings. In the wrong kind, lacking living structure, freedom of the spirit can be destroyed or weakened. If I am right, this will suggest that the character of the physical world has impact on possibly the most precious attribute of human existence. It is precisely life—the living structure of the environment—which has *this* effect.

Later he summarizes by stating, "In an environment which has living structure each of us tends, more easily, to become alive."

As mentioned above, the architecture of a building can support a community of belonging in the design of its walls, ceilings, hallways, reception areas, training and community rooms, eating spaces, meeting rooms, accommodations for food, breakout areas, and small gathering spaces. This does not even get into the design of work spaces, which I am not dealing with, as it is such well-covered territory.

The distinction to be made here is between great design that supports community, relatedness, a feeling of belonging, and great design that is about modernity, newness, and someone's legacy, which means it is usually indifferent or strictly utilitarian with respect to human habitation. Michael Freedman, an urban architect and planner, can show award-winning building designs that no one wants to inhabit and award-winning landscape designs that keep people from congregating and have no relationship to their neighborhood. This is a stunning reality. How could we design buildings and communal spaces that are not friendly to their inhabitants? Not so stunning perhaps when you realize that we design institutions, social structures, and gatherings that have the same effect.

Here is the bigger point. The buildings and material forms that we create are an outgrowth of our social fabric and capacity to be in community together. They do, in turn, impact powerfully our experience and relation to each other, but at the moment of design they are an outcome of who we are.

Alienated and retributive cultures will create alienated and unfriendly buildings and public spaces. Patriarchal institutions will create physical space that glorifies those who lead them and the designers they choose, and they will be indifferent, in the name of cost, to the space dedicated to workers and citizens. This means we must be thoughtful about the quality of relatedness that exists among those designing our spaces, for if they are at odds with each other, that is the kind of structure they will choose. One where conflicts are unresolved, isolation is glorified, and transparency is ignored.

Example: Citizen-Driven Design

Here is an example of how the planning process can involve citizens and increase the chances that the built environment will be friendly to community and belonging. In the world of community planning and landscape design, Ken Cunningham and his partner, John Spencer, have created a design process very much in line with the thinking offered here. They know that the quality of a plan is not just in the rightness of its design. The quality and success of a plan also need to be an authentic expression of the voices of the citizens who will occupy that space. The essence of their process is to invite citizens to walk, observe, and imagine what the space might become.

Every planning process claims to involve citizens and potential occupants, but in most cases it is lip service, holding to the belief that experts, usually from out of town, hold the real key to great design.

Ken and John treat citizens as producers of the design rather than as consumers who react and respond to the decisions of community leadership groups and planning experts.

The following are some elements of their thinking that fit well with the themes in this book:

- Ken and John work hard to get a cross-section of people, especially those citizens that are typically disengaged. They actively recruit those on the margin and make sure they are welcome. They want two kinds of people in the room: those who have a direct stake in the design, whom they name the "internal community," and some outsiders, whom they call the "external supportive community." This recognizes that the wider community has a stake in the quality of design for each property or neighborhood. It takes a region to raise a village.

- Before getting involved in the design, Ken and John have the citizens get to know each other. They have them meet in small groups and engage in many of the conversations for transforming community. They talk about the crossroads facing this project, they discuss their doubts and reservations, and they do the gifts conversation and name the promises they are willing to make to ensure that this project succeeds.

- Ken and John then identify several critical places in the property or neighborhood where the design will determine the essential experience of those who will eventually occupy the space. They have citizens physically walk these spots, and they ask them some interesting questions:
  - When I look at this spot, what do I see?
  - When I look, what do I know?
  - When I look, what are my assumptions?
  - When I look, what do I envision?

  These questions, asked early, evoke the imagination of those who will live with the design. This is different from creating designs or plans that express the imagination of the expert.

- After walking the physical spaces, Ken and John bring people together to post their answers to the questions. They are careful to record each comment exactly as spoken so that all ideas are held and documented. A primary goal is for citizens to recognize their contribution in the final plan. At each stage Ken and John can point to the language and words that came from citizens.

It is after the conversation with citizens that Ken and John do the traditional research and define the core elements and requirements facing the design.

Citizens are then brought together again and presented with an organized version of their comments and the results of the research. In this meeting, Ken and John use some creative ways to sustain ownership and commitment:

- In small groups they use a talking stick, which ensures that every person's voice is heard and prevents the more verbal people from dominating the conversation.

- They have designed a physical game in which people can explore and discover their choices. People place objects, buildings, benches, parks, and all the other design specifics on the board and then talk through the trade-offs in the design process. Experts usually do this; here, citizens do it.

When strong differences become obvious, they also handle conflict in a special way. They avoid the arbitrator role and instead use a fishbowl structure to resolve conflicts. They put those who disagree in the center of a group and have chairs for others to occupy so that their voices can be heard. This means other citizens participate in conflict resolution instead of the usual approach of handing the issue to a professional.

When people get stuck in their differences, Ken intervenes. He tells them, and other citizens who are interested, that they have 20 minutes to resolve the conflict. At the end of the time, Ken comes over with a pink pearl or a silver dagger. One of the two is placed on the design, depending on whether the citizens have been able to reach agreement. If they can agree, they get the pink pearl. If not, a silver dagger is placed on the design and the group moves on. He reports that this structure often achieves agreement, even when people have been at odds with each other for years.

The simple but elegant device of Ken and John's game keeps citizens engaged and treats each design question as a challenge that the community has the capacity to resolve. It also moves differences from an abstract discussion of beliefs to concrete and certain terms on paper, which is cheap.

The final step is to document what has been developed in a draft design, which is presented back to the citizens. They gather to review the design and experience the product of their efforts.

In a traditional planning process, experts do most of the work. Citizens are usually asked what they want in the design, and then the experts come up with a draft design that is presented to the citizens for feedback. The experts take the feedback back to their office and prepare a final design, which is then proposed to decision makers. There is little attention paid to creating more relatedness among stakeholders. There is no structure to have conflicts resolved by the advocates themselves. Making sure that citizens can identify where their own ideas show up in the design is left to chance. The real difference between what Ken and John do and what is traditionally done is really a contrast between the contexts out of which designers operate. Ken and John bring a context of valuing the gifts of citizens, the importance of engagement, and the hospitality of physical space, all elements of restorative places.

There Is More Than Enough Time and Just Enough Money

A final comment on space: The argument against great design is always cost and speed. The discussion about cost and speed is not really about cost and speed. It is an agenda that declares that human experience is a low priority. The argument against the importance of the aesthetic is an argument against human freedom. Low-cost and quickly constructed buildings and spaces become warehouses designed to keep under one roof and under control those people whom we do not value. We measure their value in dollars and economy. We have too often seen the construction of ugly spaces and buildings in the name of cost, or of saving taxpayers' dollars. It is not about the money. When a hallowed institution like a sports franchise or a large employer threatens to move out of town, we have all the money that is needed.

Don't ever take the argument about no funds and no time at face value. Our stance about cost and speed is simply a measure of our commitment. In every case, low cost and fast action are really an argument against the dignity of citizens and a more democratic and humanly inclusive process.

CHAPTER 15

The End of
Unnecessary Suffering

I would like to conclude with a discussion about a future that I know to be possible.

As is often said, you only teach what you need to learn, and so it is my own desire for community, my own sense of isolation and unbelonging, that have driven me into the work that has led to this book. Much of my life has been lived on the margin, outside of community, and so I am first-hand familiar with the toll it takes on a human being. This began so long ago that I have only a dim memory of its ever being any other way. Besides, any explanation I come up with would only be story. In the last ten years I have tiptoed cautiously, even reluctantly, toward fuller membership and belonging to the place where I reside, Cincinnati.

The possibility that is working on me is the reconciliation of community. Reconciliation is for me the possibility of the end of unnecessary suffering. This is the context within which I show up, even though, as with us all, I sometimes don't know whether I am working for God or the devil.

As I work to create the reconciliation and end to suffering that I am committed to, the extent of the pain running through our communities keeps commanding my attention. I want to make a distinction about this pain—it is the difference between human and political suffering. Human suffering is the pain that is inherent in being alive: isolation, loneliness, illness, abandonment, loss of meaning, sadness, and finally (I think) death.

These are unavoidable; they going to happen to each of us, and try as we may, there is nothing we can do to prevent them. We have infinite choice how to respond to this kind of human suffering, but it is part of the deal and is what gives vitality, meaning, and texture to a life.

The other kind of pain is political suffering. This is avoidable and unnecessary suffering. Some of the avoidable suffering is very visible: poverty, homelessness, hunger, violence, the diaspora of those unable to return to their homeland, a deteriorated housing project, or a neighborhood in distress. There is also political suffering that is more subtle: people's learned dependency, internalized oppression, the absence of possibility, the powerlessness that breeds violence, imperialism, and a disregard for the worth of a human being. I am calling this political suffering because I believe it grows out of human choice. Human choice to sustain a world of imbalance—surplus on one side and great scarcity on the other. This is a political choice, but not political in an electoral sense. It is not politics as in conservative or liberal, left or right. I am referring to politics as the choices we make about the distribution of power and control, and the mindset that underlies those choices.

After all the social scientists, historians, economists, biologists, and experts from other disciplines have finished with their explanations, it seems that what I am calling political, avoidable, suffering occurs as a result of our disconnectedness and the imbalance of power and resources that is such a dominant feature of our culture. This in no way puts blame on anyone or any segment of society. I do not believe "those people" exist anywhere in the world. I have simply come to believe that when we are unrelated to those whose lives are so different from ours, suffering increases.

When we see a growing distance between economic classes, an increase in protectionism and gatedness, and more resources coming into fewer hands, our capacity to bring those on the margin into the center is reduced. This is not just about large societal movements; it is also about our growing dependence on experts, our attraction to celebrity and power, our increasing tendency to label and come up with new diagnostic categories in which to pour more services. All of this is rationalized in the name of cost control and greater expertise. These are what I consider the real politics of our lives. Where does choice reside, who decides, and at what moment is the interest of the larger whole given voice?

The political suffering will decrease as we collectively choose to be together in a way that creates a space for something new to occur. What is needed is for us to choose over and over to more widely distribute ownership and account-ability. These choices will spring from the hands of citizens, rather than the hands of experts and system executives. These choices will arise when we value, invest in, and recognize the gifts and capacities of citizens.

We have evidence that this is possible and works. If you are doubtful, look at all the research on what constitutes a high-performing team; examine the employee involvement and customer service movement of the '80s and early '90s and how it helped bring U.S. companies back from the edge of irrelevance. Look at the decentralized operation of the mega-churches of today and the way the armed services have long been interested in empow-erment and point-of-contact decision making. In each of these efforts, exist-ing leadership took the initiative, and citizens and employees and members accepted their role in producing an alternative future.

Therefore, I want to end with description of how shifting our thinking and practice about the politics of experience can achieve reconciliation in several dimensions of community that are the source of so much grief:

Youth

Youth are a unifying force in community. Hard to argue against the next generation. An alternative future opens when we shift our view of youth (say 14 to 24 years old) from problem to possibility, from deficiency to gift. When you drive by a street corner and see young people hanging out at odd hours making a living in odd ways, we can view them as having gifts waiting to be given, rather than being problems waiting to be solved.

If you notice that they are dealing drugs, you hold the thought that they have entrepreneurial skill; it is just aimed in the wrong direction. If you are concerned that they are not in school, well, they are learning something, just not what we had in mind.

Someone recently said that for youth who have dropped out of school and who have no support system around them, the street corner is the only classroom that welcomes them and is available to them. It has no entrance requirements and is open 24 hours a day. Is this way of thinking true? Not exactly, but it is useful because it puts us in a more forgiving stance.

If we care about youth instead of trying to control and inculcate them, then we have to deal with our adultism. This means we have to change the nature of our listening. Create places and people that welcome youth, where youth see themselves reflected in those who have chosen to work with them.

In a youth forum recently, ten young men in their late teens were asked if they knew a white person they could trust. One raised his hand. They were asked how many owned guns. You know the answer. How many had had a friend killed in the last two years. All raised their hands.

This reality most often leads to more conversations about programs on diversity, more action on weapons, or more vigilance. A new conversation would be to focus not on the suffering in their lives, but on getting to know who these young men are, much like the Hoxseys and Sparoughs did in Findley House. To see them as gifts and capacities. These men are entrepreneurial, they are leaders among their peers, they have a strong survival instinct, they are interesting and valuable human beings and have a hunger for this to be known about them. Let us just focus on that for a while and discover what emerges. Also, they are a reflection of the world we have helped create, so a conversation about our contribution to the plight of some of our youth would make a difference. This is not about guilt, it is about our accountability.

Public Safety

The shift is to believe that citizens have the capacity to create a safe neighborhood. It is street life and connected neighbors that make a neighborhood safe. We think the police can keep us safe. In our concern for safety, we too often defer to the professionals. Police are not the answer. They are needed for crime; they cannot produce safety.

There is in every neighborhood structures for citizens to volunteer: Citizens on Patrol, Neighborhood Watch, safety meetings, educational pamphlets hung on people's front doors by the police. These go under the title of crime prevention. They are a useful warning system and help us watch out for criminals, loitering, strangers hanging out in the neighborhood, but they still function within the retributive mindset.

The shift is to realize that safety occurs through neighborhood relatedness. The efforts that move in this direction focus on identifying neighborhood assets. On creating occasions for citizens to know each other through clean-up campaigns, block parties, and citizen activist movements to confront irresponsible landlords, and abandoned houses and lots. Anything that helps neighbors to know who lives on the street. Every neighborhood has certain connector people who know everyone else's goings on. My street has Laura. She knows everyone, is on the street all the time walking dogs, caring for animals regardless of their owner, and generally providing the glue for all of us. She is the de facto Mayor of Bishop Street. We need ways to recognize these people and others.

> Sidewalk contacts are the small change from which the wealth of public life may grow.
>
> Jane Jacobs

If we looked at the assets of the neighborhood, we would realize that youth are on the streets in the afternoon, and retired people and shut-ins have the time to watch what is going on. When we recognize the gifts of these people, safety will be produced.

Development and the Local Economy

One of the largest divides in our cities is between the business community and the social activists. The activists want to protect the residents of disinvested neighborhoods. They want to make sure that lower-income residents are not pushed out of their homes or their way of life. The business community wants more home ownership and a lively area to attract professionals and cultural creatives, empty nesters, gays, and lifestyle enthusiasts. The future is named development by the businesses and gentrification by the activists. This puts the social activists and developers at odds with each other. The argument needs reframing. In most places, either it either stays an impasse, or the developers, with the help of local government and tax benefits from the federal government, carry the day.

It is a polarized conversation, with low trust and each side attached to its story. Developers bemoan the social services concentrated in poorer neighborhoods. Activists know that without a strong voice, the poor will be sent to warehouses under the interstate highway.

Reconciliation will occur through a new conversation where the developers talk about the compassion they hold for those on the margin. The new conversation for the social activists is to acknowledge that without some wealth coming into their neighborhoods, they will continue to depopulate and deteriorate. The way into a different future is to build relatedness between these groups. Beneath their positions is a common concern for the well-being of the city. A perpetually wounded city serves no one's concerns. There are many examples where these groups have come together. It is all possible when people decide to work something out rather than trying to win and being right. It is the shift in conversation and a care for the whole that makes the difference.

The other monster issue facing the country and community is the development of a local economy. Small businesses are the growth engine that is kind to community. Each neighborhood has a micro-economy that needs to be healthy. A place where people live, work, and shop. Most of the visible models are for well-off, resurgent neighborhoods. The emergent possibility is to create neighborhoods that are vital and friendly to the middle class. This is also the way out for those on the margin. For example, a strong local African-American economy does more to create racial justice than minority hiring regulations and diversity workshops.

Jim Clingman, an active citizen of Cincinnati, has given voice to this issue for years. He calls it Blackonomics. Find his books and read them. He argues that the civil rights movement created political freedom for blacks to live, vote, and shop according to their wants, but this occurred at the expense of the economic well-being of African-American small-business owners. This becomes the new conversation. How to marry capital with all the educational opportunities for creating business plans and incubator agencies that are intended to expand the pool of entrepreneurs. The answer for those on the margin is to become economically self-sufficient. Working at minimum-wage service jobs or becoming acculturated to work for mainstream large businesses leaves too many young people outside the living wage economy.

One more point. We need to educate people about the politics of the dollar. When they shop at the big box stores, searching for the lowest cost, they do this at the expense of the community and local economy. For every dollar they save at the big boxes, they spend a dollar fifty in taxes, high-interest loans for credit cards, overpriced staples at convenience stores, and get-me-through-the-night loan operations. Supporting small businesses, buying from those people who are a reflection of who you are, circulates money among businesses that will be ultimately sustaining. Hard message to get across with the avalanche of advertising, *Baywatch* desires, and BET and Nike models of the good life. If we do not become conscious of the political and economic power of a single dollar, the class divide will only widen.

Family Well-Being and Human Services

In the human services world, we intend to approach families as whole systems; we talk about integrating service but are so broken into disciplines and accreditations that it is mostly lip service. Even if we did organize services around the family, we are still deficiency oriented.

To fully explore this is beyond our purpose here, but a couple of headlines will make the point. The shift in framing is that people and families are a pool of gifts and capacities, not a series of needs and deficiencies. Their suffering is an effect of their isolation and their being labeled. The struggle in their life is to find a way to use their gifts. In the way we traditionally deliver service, by raising money for and valuing their deficiencies, we reflect and reinforce the cause of some of their troubles.

We still call citizens who seek help "cases." People who serve them are called "case workers." What does it means when someone is labeled a "case"? Lawyers, social workers, human service workers in general dehumanize those they are committed to serve by naming them cases.

Human services also relate to citizens through diagnostic categories. We are only interested in their needs and deficiencies. If a family or person has no pressing needs and deficiencies, nothing that can be categorized, we have no interest in them. Perhaps we should develop diagnostic categories for people's gifts. Right now we have only crude positive labels: high school graduate, economic status, size of family, job experience. Suppose we named people in categories, such as: a connector, knows everyone in the neighborhood, street-level entrepreneur, fashion plate, compassion for those in need, lights up a room when they enter, creative speech, practical intelligence, risk taker.

The shift is to focus on gifts and capacities. Again, McKnight has led the way in this thinking.

Example: Cynthia Smith

Cynthia Smith is assistant director of client services at the Hamilton County Department of Job and Family Services. They service about 30,000 citizens through the front door per month. Cynthia decided to work at shifting the thinking of her division from the needs of people to the gifts of people. She got interested in something called Appreciative Inquiry, which is a way of helping institutions to build a future on what is positive about their past and present. It is designed to use appreciation as a form of leadership and organization development. According to some, this is a radical path for human services.

In addition to exploring an appreciative way of bettering performance, Cynthia also had the consciousness that the employees of Job and Family Services (JFS) reflect in their own lives the same struggles and heartaches of the general population that JFS is chartered to serve. This means that if we want to transform the context and thinking of those we are here to serve, then we must begin with ourselves. The internal culture of a human services system must value the gifts and capacities of its own employees before those employees can bring that mindset to the community. People inside systems need to operate with compassion and appreciation toward each other. To recognize that the struggles of those we serve exist within us. This consciousness is the antidote to the tendency to be patronizing toward those who seek our services. How can we be hospitable to the community if we are not hospitable to each other?

Cynthia has initiated this internal inquiry in collaboration with other staff initiatives. She has not constructed it as a system change program, but as a way of giving leadership to her own division.

Another important step she has taken is to invite members of the community at large to be part of the internal conversations she is initiating. She values the capacity of the larger village to care for the success of JFS, which is radical and healing in itself. Most government agencies think they have to defend and justify themselves to the community; Cynthia welcomes the community in, to help create an alternative and more restorative future. She believes it does take a village to raise a child and is acting on it.

Health Care

Health care ranks high on centralized control, private sector domination, and dependency on expert intervention. We thought that merger and restructuring health care would help. We moved to managed care and brought 60 percent of the physicians under that umbrella. We privatized with all the bottom-line efficiency that promised. We have invested heavily in research and dramatized the heroism of the professional. There are few industries that are more regulated.

Health care also ranks high on every dimension for the conventional wisdom about how transformation occurs. Strong leadership, noble vision, clear outcomes, predictable and regulated practices, tight measures, high influence expertise, major investment in training.

So, how is it going?

Not great. The United States spends 40 percent more on health care than the next high-spending nation, Switzerland. Yet the average rank in quality of care and health of citizens in the United States doesn't quite make it into the top ten.

What is paradoxical is that all who work in health care are committed, well-intentioned human beings. What is poignant is that most who work in the system, these committed, caring people, agree that the system is not working. Some call it broken.

For anything important to shift, context needs to shift. The current context is a conversation about cost control and access (which is argued as a cost issue). This conversation is about minor improvements, making what is not working cheaper and more available. These conversations will not create an alternative future. To oversimplify, we are asking the wrong questions.

The current conversation about controlling costs is not changing the nature of the system. There is little discussion about changing the way care is delivered. Little discussion about changing our thinking about care, and who is responsible for our health.

For example, we have only begun to shift to a focus on health versus disease. The profession is very tentative about taking seriously nonchemical forms of healing (which the profession would name as nonexpert intervention). In fact, anyone who focuses on anything other than system care, professional knowing, and chemical treatment is called alternative medicine. As if we would never turn to it first, only as an alternative. It is as if the conversation about prevention, widely available curatives, healthy eating, positive life style habits, and ancient and traditional healing were not medicine, but a second cousin. As if we had to choose between alternatives. Pick one or the other. And if you want your insurance company to pay for your getting healthy, you know which one gets the nod.

I want to end with two examples of what inverted thinking and relatedness look like in the world. These are two stories of individuals taking a stand for a possibility. They have organized their practice as an example of a future, and done so at significant personal cost, with the belief that local action, committed to over a long period of time, is how the world changes. And they do this in an industry where most feel helpless about anything really changing. Not these two.

Example: Paul Uhlig

A thoracic heart surgeon named Paul Uhlig is opening new possibilities for health care. In many ways he is creating an alternative future for his calling. He has been very innovative in the realm of collaborative care and the value of collaborative rounds. Collaborative rounds, in Paul's practice, are where the physician, nurse, social worker, and other support people working with a patient literally stand in a circle with the patient and his or her family and talk together about the patient's condition and path of action. This means that decisions will be based on more than just the progress of the disease; they will include the viewpoints of the whole team, patient and family included. This is in sharp contrast to the common practice of placing the decisions about care in the hands of the single expert, the physician, or a team of experts. The idea that the patient, family, social workers, and nurses have a voice about care, expressed in front of all others, is a serious inversion of thinking. From physician as the cause of care shifting to the patient and care community. If you do not realize how radical this is, get thee to a hospital.

Collaborative care has been around for some time and was not invented by Paul and his team, but they have moved it forward with their advocacy. They have accumulated hard evidence on the impact of this kind of collaborative care, with data on the improvement in patient safety, length of stay in the hospital, patient and family satisfaction, and professional satisfaction. With the collaborative methodology, all these measures improve, at little increase in cost. If a drug were developed that produced one half of the outcomes that this innovation has produced, it would be used in every system in the country.

In the face of this, Paul has been treated by his industry as an interesting anomaly in the system. As a surgeon he is near the top of the food chain. Still, wherever he goes, he both draws interest and catalyzes resistance. The problem is that Paul's innovation confronts the dominance of the expert model in the extreme. And it delivers no large profits to the institution.

Paul believes that a community of care is what will make the difference in our health. Ninety-five percent of his heart surgery patients will return to the lifestyle that broke their heart after the professional supports, which are very expensive, have disappeared. The 5 percent who do change their lives hold on to this commitment by working with others to do the same.

What Paul is paying attention to gives an indication of the shift in conversation that might lead to real transformation in the health care industry. The new conversation he is initiating is one of *ownership*. What is our individual and community contribution to the problems we are facing? What *commitment* am I as a citizen willing to make toward my own health? What is the *possibility* of creating wellness in the world rather than fighting disease? What is the *refusal* I am willing to make to the expert and professional control of the conventional solutions? Collaborative rounds is a means for creating a new conversation that places the doctor, the family, the supporting professionals, and the patient all at the center of the planning and decision-making process.

Making these questions central would shift the nature of the health care debate. This conversation would change the context from disease to health, from romance with technology and drugs to actions on the part of the citizen, from discussions of cost control and dependence on the professional to engaging the community.

Example: Dorothy Shaffer

One more example of how transformation happens small, quietly, in rooms designed for humans and based on relatedness. Dr. Dorothy Shaffer is a Cincinnati physician in internal medicine. I first noticed she was up to something before I met her. Most mornings I take the kids to school and drive through a neighborhood somewhat on the edge. I noticed on the corner of Reading and Clinton Springs the renovation of an old house that was taking forever. What were they doing there, why was it taking so long; strange neighborhood to make that kind of investment. Then forgot about it.

Two years later I am shopping for a new physician. A friend recommends Dr. Shaffer, who I find out was the one who renovated that building I had been watching. When I go there, I realize she has taken the care to create a version of the possibility of health care. Here is a taste of the future, on the corner of Reading and Clinton Springs.

You call for an appointment and a human being answers the phone. I ask for an appointment and she apologizes that I will have to wait three weeks, since I am a new patient. She asks why I want to see the doctor. Tells me that if I become a patient, there will be a $250 annual fee. I agree to this. This is to enable Dr. Shaffer to keep her patient load down to give the service she wants to give. For those who cannot afford the fee, she waives it or figures out what will be possible for that patient.

I show up for my appointment and walk into a living room. It's like staying at a W Hotel, where they redesigned the lobby as a living room. I go to the desk and on the counter there are raisins, not candy and not nothing. The receptionist gives me forms to complete, and when I am done, she says the doctor will be right with me. I sit down and see there are books with some intellectual content: poetry, the environment, nontraditional cures. I have to search hard for *People* and *Time* magazines, both of which are entertaining and content free.

With too little time to catch up on national gossip, I am brought right away to the examining room. The nurse takes my vital signs and weighs me *without* my shoes on. Scale is a little inaccurate on the heavy side, but not to be picky.

I am not asked to take any clothes off. There is not the embarrassment and vulnerability of changing clothes for the sake of strangers. Doctor comes in without a clinical coat. Dressed casually in street clothes. We talk, she does the exam, is not anxious about the time. Is interested in my way of eating, lifestyle, stress in my life (takes a while). She knows about vitamins, supplements and explains why some are better than others. She thinks part of her job is to educate me.

She is more interested in the person than disease. Most of her focus is on keeping me healthy. Exercise and diet are major focuses for her. Everyone's body resists certain foods, and she suggests we find out about mine. Her office offers acupuncture, massage, and other healing arts, all in the same building. She has organized her service around the patient. I now have one physician who sees the whole picture, one place that treats the whole person.

Dr. Shaffer has eliminated the distinction between conventional and alternative medicine. She has put the patient at the center of the service. She has transformed health care.

If there are people like Paul Uhlig and Dotty Shaffer in one community, then we know there are others like them in all communities. All we have to do is recognize them, support them, and declare them to be mainstream.

Book at a Glance

This section is a quick summary and reference guide to the book. You are welcome to copy and use at will. First come the context and main ideas. Next is a summary of the questions. Finally is a quick look at designing the physical space.

Overall Premise

Build the social fabric and transform the isolation within our communities into connectedness and caring for the whole.

Shift our conversations from the problems of community to the possibility of community.

Commit to create a future distinct from the past.

Operating Guidelines

Social fabric is created one room at a time, the one we are in at the moment.

It is formed out of the questions "Whom do we want in the room?" and "What is the new conversation that we want to occur?"

The key to a new future is to focus on gifts, on associational life, and on the insight that all transformation occurs through language.

Each step has to embody a quality of aliveness, and strategy evolves in an organic way.

The essence of creating an alternative future comes from citizen-to-citizen engagement that constantly focuses on the well-being of the whole.

We have all the capacity, expertise, and financial resources that an alternative future requires.

The small group is the unit of transformation and the container for the experience of belonging.

The Context for a Restorative Community

The existing community context is one that markets fear, assigns fault, and worships self-interest.

This context supports the belief that the future will be improved with new laws, more oversight, and stronger leadership.

The new context that restores community is one of possibility, generosity, and gifts, rather than one of fear, mistakes, and self-interest.

Citizens become powerful when they choose to shift the context within which they act in the world.

Communities are human systems given form by conversations that build relatedness.

The conversations that build relatedness most often occur through associational life, where citizens are unpaid and show up by choice, rather than in large systems where professionals are paid and show up by contractual agreement.

The future hinges on the accountability that citizens choose and their willingness to connect with each other around promises they make to each other.

Citizens have the capacity to own and exercise power rather than defer or delegate it to others.

The Inversion of Cause and Accountability

We reclaim our citizenship when we invert what is cause and what is effect.

Citizens create leaders, children create parents, and audience creates the performance. This inversion may not be the whole truth, but it is useful.

The inversion creates conditions where we can shift from

A place of fear and fault to one of gifts, generosity, and abundance;

A bet on law and oversight to one on social fabric and chosen accountability;

The corporation and systems as central, to associational life as central;

A focus on leaders to a focus on citizens;

Problems to possibility.

Leadership and Transformation

Leadership that engages citizens is a capacity that exists in all human beings. It is infinitely and universally available.

Transformation occurs when leaders focus on the structure of how we gather and the context in which the gatherings take place.

Leadership is convening and held to three tasks:

Shift the context within which people gather.

Name the debate through powerful questions.

Listen rather than advocate, defend, or provide answers.

The Power of the Small Group

Each gathering needs to become an example of the future we want to create.

The small group is the unit of transformation.

Large-scale transformation occurs when enough small groups shift in harmony toward the larger change.

Small groups have the most leverage when they meet as part of a larger gathering.

The small group produces power when diversity of thinking and dissent are given space, commitments are made without barter, and the gifts of each person and our community are acknowledged and valued.

Questions Are More Transforming Than Answers

The skill is getting the questions right.

The traditional conversations that seek to explain, study, analyze, define tools, and express the desire to change others are interesting but not powerful.

Questions open the door to the future and are more powerful than answers in that they demand engagement. Engagement in the right questions is what creates accountability.

How we frame the questions is decisive. They need to be ambiguous, personal, and stressful.

Introduce the questions by defining the distinction the question addresses, namely what is different and unique about this conversation.

We need to inoculate people against advice and help. Advice is replaced by curiosity.

The Invitation

Invite people who are not used to being together.

The elements of a powerful invitation:

Name the possibility about which we are convening.

Specify what is required of each should they choose to attend.

Make the invitation as personal as possible.

Be clear that a refusal carries no cost.

The Questions

The five conversations for structuring belonging are possibility, ownership, dissent, commitment, and gifts.

Since all the conversations lead to each other, sequence is not that critical.

Create conversations in ascending order of difficulty, with possibility generally an early conversation and gifts typically one of the more difficult.

There are three elements of a question:

The distinction that underlies the question.

An admonition against advice and help and in favor of curiosity.

The question itself, stated precisely.

The Possibility Conversation

The distinction is between possibility and problem solving. Possibility is a future beyond reach.

The possibility conversation works on us and evolves from a discussion of personal crossroads. It takes the form of a declaration, best made publicly.

The Questions

What is the crossroads you are faced with at this point in time?

What declaration of possibility can you make that has the power to transform the community and inspire you?

The Ownership Conversation

It asks citizens to act as if they are creating what exists in the world.

The distinction is between ownership and blame.

The Questions

For an event or project:

How valuable an experience (or project, or community) do you plan for this to be?

How much risk are you willing to take?

How participative do you plan to be?

To what extent are you invested in the well-being of the whole?

The all-purpose ownership question:

What have I done to contribute to the very thing I complain about or want to change?

The questions that can complete our story and remove its limiting quality:

What is the story about this community or organization that you hear yourself most often telling? The one you are wedded to and maybe even take your identity from?

What are the payoffs you receive from holding on to this story?

What is your attachment to this story costing you?

The Dissent Conversation

The dissent conversation creates an opening for commitment.

When dissent is expressed, just listen. Don't solve it, defend against it, or explain anything.

The primary distinction is between dissent and lip service.

A second distinction is between dissent and denial, rebellion, or resignation.

The Questions

What doubts and reservations do you have?

What is the no or refusal that you keep postponing?

What have you said yes to that you no longer really mean?

What is a commitment or decision that you have changed your mind about?

What resentment do you hold that no one knows about?

What forgiveness are you withholding?

The Commitment Conversation

The commitment conversation is a promise with no expectation of return.

Commitment is distinguished from barter.

The enemy of commitment is lip service, not dissent or opposition.

The commitments that count the most are ones made to peers, other citizens.

We have to explicitly provide support for citizens to declare that there is no promise they are willing to make at this time.

Refusal to promise does not cost us our membership or seat at the table. We only lose our seat when we do not honor our word.

Commitment embraces two kinds of promises:

My behavior and actions with others

Results and outcomes that will occur in the world

The Questions

What promises am I willing to make?

What measures have meaning to me?

What price am I willing to pay?

What is the cost to others for me to keep my commitments, or to fail in my commitments?

What is the promise I'm willing to make that constitutes a risk or major shift for me?

What is the promise I am postponing?

What is the promise or commitment I am unwilling to make?

The Gifts Conversation

The leadership and citizen task is to bring the gifts of those on the margin into the center.

The distinction is between gifts and deficiencies or needs.

We are not defined by deficiencies or what is missing. We are defined by our gifts and what is present.

We choose our destiny when we have the courage to acknowledge our own gifts and choose to bring them into the world.

A gift is not a gift until it is offered.

The Questions

What is the gift you still hold in exile?

What is something about you that no one knows?

What gratitude do you hold that has been gone unexpressed?

What have others in this room done, in this gathering, that has touched you?

Final Comment

The important thing about these questions is that they name the agenda that creates space for an alternative future. The power is in the asking, not in the answers.

Designing Physical Space That Supports Community

Physical space is more decisive in creating community than we realize.

Most meeting spaces are designed for control, negotiation, and persuasion.

We always have a choice about how we rearrange and occupy whatever room we are handed.

Community is built when we sit in circles, when there are windows and the walls have signs of life, when every voice can be equally heard and amplified, when we all are on one level—and the chairs have wheels and swivel.

When we have an opportunity to design new space, we need the following:

Reception areas that tell us we are in the right place and are welcome.

Hallways wide enough for intimate seating and casual contact.

Eating spaces that refresh us and encourage relatedness.

Meeting rooms designed with nature, art, conviviality, and citizen-to-citizen interaction in mind.

Large community spaces that have the qualities of communal intimacy.

The design process itself needs to be an example of the future we are intending to create.

Authentic citizen and employee engagement is as important as good design expertise.

Role Models and Resources

In what is traditionally a place for books and references, I want to add citizens who are bringing their gifts into their communities. In every community there are tens of thousands of people who build that community, not because it is their job, but because of who they are. These are the major players of associational life. Here I have listed a very few that I am familiar with, just to hold a place in this book for this special kind of citizen. Unfortunately, I have left out many more than mentioned, so I ask their forgiveness for this.

Alexander, Christopher

In their words: "Our goal is to help everyone make our neighborhoods places of belonging, places of health and well-being, and places where people will want to live and work. This has become possible through the use of Generative Codes, Christopher Alexander's latest work in the effort to make possible conception and construction of living, beautiful communities that have real guts—not the sugary sweetness of pseudo-traditional architecture.

"The tools offered are intended for the use of ordinary people, families, communities, developers, planners, architects, designers, and builders; public officials, local representatives, and neighbors; business owners and people who have commercial interests. The processes here are expressed in the belief that the common-sense, plain truth about laying out a neighborhood, or repairing one, is equally valid for all comers, amateurs and professionals.

They help people build or rebuild neighborhoods in ways that contribute something to their lives. Many of the tools have their origin in 30 years of work published in Alexander's *The Nature of Order.*"

The Timeless Way of Building. New York: Oxford University Press, 1979.

The Nature of Order, Book 1: The Phenomenon of Life. Berkeley: Center for Environmental Structure, 2004. (Passages quoted in Chapter 1 are from pages 20 and 122.)

The Nature of Order, Book 2: The Process of Creating Life. Berkeley: Center for Environmental Structure, 2006.

The Nature of Order, Book 3: A Vision of a Living World. Berkeley: Center for Environmental Structure, 2004.

The Nature of Order, Book 4: The Luminous Ground. Berkeley: Center for Environmental Structure, 2003.

Pattern Language (www.patternlanguage.com)

Allah, Islord

Islord is one of the founders of Elementz, a Hip Hop Center for urban youth. He is now its program director and is also a musician and an entrepreneur. He stands as a beacon of strength and commitment to every young person who comes in off the street. When youths come in the door, they see in him a reflection of themselves, except he carries in him the belief that anything is possible. It is this gift of possibility that is most needed in the world he is transforming.

See **Elementz,** *below.*

Art of Hosting, The

In their words: "The art of hosting is a practice that heals the broken relationships between people. The Art of Hosting and Convening Conversations that matter is a powerful leadership practicum as well as a daily pattern and practice for many individuals, communities, families, businesses, and organizations."

The Art of Hosting (www.artofhosting.org)

A Small Group

There are countless groups in Cincinnati that want to better it one way or another—as in any good-sized city. ASG exists to widen the net of engaged citizens. Its method is to change the conversation in a way that makes this city a better place to live in. Here is its statement of purpose:

"We are committed to the creation of a restorative and reconciled community. Our strategy is to discover ways to engage the disengaged through working with existing associations and through direct invitation. Our work focuses on direct efforts to bring into conversation those groups of people who are not in relationship with each other. By this we mean to offer powerful tools and strategies of civic possibility, civic accountability, and civic commitment; thus increasing the power of associations to engage citizens in their efforts."

A Small Group (www.asmallgroup.net)

Axelrod, Dick and Emily

Dick and Emily are among the world's greatest designers of learning experience. They really know how to create high-engagement gatherings. The part of their work that does not show up in their books or teaching is that they bring a great humanity and love of democratic processes wherever they go.

In their words: "We design collaborative systems which enable leaders and workers to jointly construct a company both profitable and worthy of pride. Some have called our practices 'organizational barn raising' because the focus and energy shown by participants reminds them of the old-time, community barn raisings, in which neighbors would erect a sturdy building in a weekend."

You Don't Have to Do It Alone: How to Involve Others to Get Things Done. San Francisco: Berrett-Koehler Publishers, 2004.

Terms of Engagement: Changing the Way We Change Organizations. San Francisco: Berrett-Koehler Publishers, 2000.

The Conference Model. San Francisco: Berrett-Koehler Publishers, 2000.

The Axelrod Group (www.axelrodgroup.com)

Bornstein, David

Bornstein brings a journalist's eye and writing style to the public benefit arena. He also speaks in a quiet and compelling way about what makes a difference in civic space.

How to Change the World: Social Entrepreneurs and the Power of New Ideas. New York: Oxford University Press, 2004.

The Price of a Dream: The Story of the Grameen Bank (paper reissue). New York: Oxford University Press, 2005.

How to Change the World (www.howtochangetheworld.org)

Brook, Peter

This book is about the theater, but it is written so brilliantly, and with such wisdom and depth, that all that he says about the theater is true about a wide range of human endeavors. As I read this book, every time he said "theater," I was thinking training events, conferences, and any event designed to touch and change people's experience.

The Empty Space: A Book About the Theatre Deadly, Holy, Rough, Immediate. New York: Touchstone, 1968.

Brown, Juanita, and David Isaacs

Juanita and David have invented a large group method that is virally changing the world. It is precise, elegant, and profound.

In their words: "The World Café is an innovative yet simple methodology for hosting conversations about questions that matter. These conversations link and build on each other as people move between groups, cross-pollinate ideas, and discover new insights into the questions or issues that are most important in their life, work, or community. As a process, the World Café can evoke and make visible the collective intelligence of any group, thus increasing people's capacity for effective action in pursuit of common aims."

The World Café: Shaping Our Futures Through Conversations That Matter, with the World Café Community. San Francisco: Berrett-Koehler Publishers, 2005.

The World Café (www.theworldcafe.com)

Brundage, Theresa

Theresa has given her life to developing and running programs to support and empower those on the margin. When she walks into the room, collaboration and relatedness enter with her in a way I have seldom seen. She is one of my heroes.

See **Seven Hills Neighborhood Houses,** *below.*

Bunker, Barbara, and Billie T. Alban

Barbara and Billie have long practiced a very thoughtful, patient, and authentic form of consultation. Their writing has helped give form and legitimacy to a holistic approach to organization development.

> *The Handbook of Large Group Methods: Creating Systemic Change in Organizations and Communities.* San Francisco: Jossey-Bass, 2006.

> *Large Group Interventions: Engaging the Whole System for Rapid Change.* San Francisco: Jossey-Bass, 1997.

Burke, Tricia

Executive director of Clermont Counseling Center

The story of the Center is in the book. Tricia is the epitome of someone who has sustained a commitment to reduce suffering over a long period of time; and yet, despite the difficulties to sustain oneself in this effort, her curiosity and willingness to create something new are startling. She is still curious.

Clermont Counseling Center (www.clermontcounseling.org)

Butler, Mike

Mike has been inventing community policing for a couple of decades. He runs the police department in Longmont, Colorado, which is based on the insight that safety comes from building a strong community, with law and order as a backup strategy. Here is a recent note from him that gives a hint at what he is up to: "Our local restorative justice project has evolved to a whole different level. We are on the front end of turning our criminal justice system in our area into a restorative justice system."

Longmont Police Department (www.ci.longmont.co.us/police)

Carlsbad, California

Their description: "After celebrating our 50th anniversary as an incorporated city in 2002, the City of Carlsbad decided an important new crossroads was ahead. To take advantage of the opportunities, City leaders decided to re-think the City's past, present and future. In doing so they looked to the community to help define a vision. And so, the 'Connecting Community, Place & Spirit' mission was undertaken, guided by a team of City Council members and staff."

Also see more on City Manager **Ray Patchett,** *below.*

City of Carlsbad (www.carlsbadca.gov/ccps/index.html)

Casarez, Margaret

Mag runs the Phoenix Place program mentioned in the text in Chapter 4. She is a model of the type of citizen this book is about and written for. She plays a leadership role as a volunteer in a Cincinnati program, Invest in Neighborhoods, and has brought the new conversations into this effort with great success. If you want to know how these conversations work in new and difficult places, contact her.

Margaret Casarez (www.margaretcasarez.com)

Cass, Phil

Phil runs a health foundation and is bringing the power of the circle, the power of the small group, and the power of the art of convening to the challenge of health care in Columbus, Ohio. He is an example of a high-level community leader who is using his place in the city to initiate profound reforms in the thinking and practice of organizing citizens to reclaim their power to create the kind of health and wellness system that they want. He is working with the Art of Hosting, referenced above.

Columbus Medical Association and Foundation (www.goodhealth columbus.org)

Clingman, James

Jim is a strong voice for the importance of a black economy. He helped start an entrepreneurial school in Cincinnati, writes articles, speaks on radio and TV. He has got it right.

Blackonomic$: The Way to Psychological and Economic Freedom for African Americans. Los Angeles: Milligan Books, 2001.

Blackonomic$ (www.blackonomics.com)

Cohen, Allan

Allan is the best business strategist I know. He brings an intimate knowledge of the field of emergent design and integrates it with the social technology of possibility, group process, and creating new conversations. His work in difficult, loosely coupled organizations such as universities has produced results that you just do not come across very often. He also contributes greatly to the Mastery Foundation.

See **Ann Overton,** *below.*

Allan Cohen (www.allancohen.com)

Cooper Reed, Eileen

A former executive for the Children's Defense Fund, Eileen at this writing is president of the School Board for Cincinnati Public Schools. All of us give lip service to the importance of the next generation; Eileen gives her talent, her commitment, and her life to all of our children. She is a powerful voice for the community and has particularly been active in bringing women together in service of achieving peace in the place where she lives. She sits as grounded and comfortably in the glare of public attention as anyone I know.

Cincinnati Public Schools (www.cps-k12.org/board/bdmembers/ cooperreed)

Cornerstone Community Loan Fund

In their words: "Cornerstone revitalizes distressed urban neighborhoods from the inside out. We begin by organizing groups of low income people who are committed to improving their lives and neighborhood. Cornerstone provides professional support for cooperative efforts to develop quality affordable housing, a safe and attractive environment, and new financial resources and skills, building wealth and futures in the community."

Cornerstone Community Loan Fund (www.cornerstoneloanfund.org)

Covington, Kentucky, Center for Great Neighborhoods

In their words: "The truth is struggling neighborhoods won't improve because of a federal grant or outside resource alone. Lasting change only occurs when people take ownership of their community and their own lives. We can pave the streets and paint the houses, but unless people care about each other and the future of their community, it won't be a truly great neighborhood."

The Center for Great Neighborhoods of Covington (www.greatneighbor hoods.org)

Covrett, Donna

Donna is a connector. She remembers people. I think she likes people. She is an energy source that should be commercialized. Her reach in the community is wide, her care for others is persistent, and she is a community asset right up there with the baseball stadium. Her medium is as food editor, at this time of writing, for *Cincinnati Magazine*. She uses her commitment to food as a way of being awake and as a medium for hospitality. She denies she is a recognizable public figure, but when you go out to eat with her, the service is really good.

dcovrett@cintimag.emmis.com

Cunningham, Ken

Ken is married to John Spencer and they are true urban pioneers in Cincinnati. Their design process is mentioned in the text, and that is a small sample of the intelligence and insight they bring to the city. While they list themselves as landscape architects, they have contributed more broadly in building the social fabric of their community.

Contact Ken and John at kcai@one.net.

Dannemiller, Kathie

Kathie has passed on, but her ideas and inclusive generosity live in all she touched. She always had her mind and heart on the well-being of the whole, and has been a major influence on people concerned with bringing people together. An important teacher in my thinking and practice.

In their words: "We help people combine and focus their power, wisdom, and heart to create successful, sustainable organizations and communities. We do this by pioneering and applying whole-system approaches to learning and change."

> *Whole-Scale Change: Unleashing the Magic in Organizations.* San Francisco: Berrett-Koehler Publishers, 2000.

Dannemiller Tyson Associates (www.dannemillertyson.com)

Designed Learning

If you would like to further explore the ideas in this book, contact Designed Learning. In their words: "Designed Learning is a full-service training and consulting organization existing to help organizations succeed at complex change. Through a variety of innovative ideas and technologies, we help our client organizations support the transformation of staff people into effective internal consultants and consultant teams.

"Designed Learning has a number of learning experiences and consulting interventions that assist organizations and communities in exploring the concept of creating 'chosen accountability' and futures that are different from our past.

"Our work with The Six Conversations that Matter™ includes half-day, full-day, and two-day workshops designed to explore the linguistic changes that need to occur to create sustainable communities and organizations.

"In addition, The Flawless Consulting™ Workshops are a key element in our mission to help organizations build capacity and develop people for more successful, more meaningful work. Three hands-on, skill-building workshops are designed for internal and external consultants to learn how to establish and maintain collaborative working relations with clients, which result in positive outcomes for the business, and to learn how to have influence when you do not have control."

To learn more about these workshops and consulting services, contact

Bill Brewer
bbrewer@designedlearning.com
Phone: 513-524-2227 or 866-770-2227
E-mail: info@designedlearning.com

Designed Learning (www.designedlearning.com)

Dutton, Tim

Tim runs SCOPE and is a major connector in Sarasota, Florida. He and his staff take on the most difficult challenges, such as race, aging, and housing, and do it in a way that brings all the stakeholders into the room together. His group has been applying the conversations outlined in this book for several years. Tim's commitment to help those on the margin is unwavering, and his capacity to function at every level of society is a huge community asset. He is also a great friend.

See **SCOPE,** *below.*

Dutton, Tom

There are professors in higher education who are changing the world, and Tom is one of them. He has created a Center for Community Engagement in Cincinnati that gives real teeth to service learning. He is an architecture professor at Miami University in Oxford, Ohio. He is also an excellent thinker and writer, and is a major voice in ensuring that urban development takes into account the lives and rights of local residents. He brings architecture students from idyllic Oxford and brings them into Cincinnati to design and build in the center of the urban environment. Last summer he had nine students not only study in the center city but also live there for ten weeks. Their lives were touched in powerful ways. Those whom they had initially thought were strangers became friends. They saw the gifts of street people, and were no longer afraid of a neighborhood that has been marketed for years by the media as a place to avoid. This effort met the criteria of small scale, small group, slow pace, low budget, and high interaction. Education at its finest. Service learning as it was intended to be.

See **Miami University Center for Community Engagement,** *below.*

Elementz: Hip Hop Youth Arts Center

In their words: "The Hip Hop Youth Arts Center is a safe space, an empowering space, and a space for development. Young people ages 14–24 are one of our most untapped resources, and we provide an outlet for their expression that is a needed alternative to violence. We serve youth that either live in or come to the Over-the-Rhine/West End area—a place where people from all over the city gather. Hip Hop culture—including dj-ing, emceeing/rapping, break dancing, and graffiti art—is the center of everything we do. We believe people learn best from their experience. Hip Hop culture is what youth today come up in. We do our best to provide access to the equipment and resources necessary to grow and learn in positive ways. The Hip Hop community in Cincinnati is our biggest and best resource."

Elementz (www.natiyouthcenter.org)

Erhard, Werner

Werner has developed programs that have touched millions of lives. His work is delivered through Landmark Education and other consulting associates. I have learned from Werner what it looks like to be totally focused on reducing suffering and making a difference in people's lives. His personal generosity and willingness to engage people in strong and compassionate ways is another form that his teaching takes. His thinking has impacted every aspect of my practice and way of being.

From the Landmark Education Web site: "Whenever we're limited in life, there is something—a context or framework—that we are blind to and that is holding that limitation in place. Landmark's technology allows you to create breakthroughs in a two-step process in which you:

- Uncover and examine the blind spots or context holding you back in your life.

- Find out where your current context originated and address it for what it really is.

"Having completed these two steps, a new realm of possibility is available to you. The constraints from the past disappear. Your view of life, your thoughts, your feelings, and your actions, change—and the change is immediate, dramatic, and without effort. It is a breakthrough."

Erhard, Werner, Michael C. Jensen, and Steve Zaffron. *Integrity: Where Leadership Begins—A New Model of Integrity (PDF File of PowerPoint Slides)* (June 18, 2007). Barbados Group Working Paper No. 07-03. Available at SSRN: http://ssrn.com/abstract=983401.

Erhard, Werner, Michael C. Jensen, and Steve Zaffron. *Integrity: A Positive Model That Incorporates the Normative Phenomena of Morality, Ethics, and Legality (PDF File of Keynote Slides)* (August 24, 2007). Barbados Group Working Paper No. 06-07. Available at SSRN: http://ssrn.com/abstract=932255.

Landmark Education (www.landmark-education.com)

Friends of Werner Erhard (www.wernererhard.com)

Erpenbeck, Joe

Joe works in the disabilities world for a large county board. Within this system he has created a small team of people who are moving from providing services to building community. In his case, community is built around individuals whom we used to call the "disabled." His group is alert to people's gifts, their desires, and what makes them happy. They then find ways that these gifts can be offered, whether through a hobby, an interest, or just the willingness to be in the room with a group of strangers. Joe's project has radical implications for social service, and he has results to show for it.

Hamilton County Board of Mental Retardation and Developmental Disabilities (www.hamiltonmrdd.org)

Everett, Ed

Former city manager, Redwood City, California

Ed is a progressive city manager who decided a few years ago that stronger civic engagement was part of the legacy he wanted to leave behind. What follows is an excerpt from an award he received that expresses his gifts better than I could:

"The International City/County Management Association (ICMA) has awarded its most-prestigious annual award, the *Award for Career Excellence*, to Ed Everett, City Manager of Redwood City. . . . Mr. Everett has dedicated his career to going beyond the standard of working toward 'just' a well-managed city government; instead, he has set the standard for new heights of community involvement and engagement, and inspired a genuine dedication in staff and in elected officials. During his tenure as City Manager, a number of ground-breaking Community Building programs were developed, and have matured into respected, valued, and sought-after elements contributing to our community's quality of life; other cities have used this model to provide similar programs—Partnership Academy for Community Teamwork, Community Builders speakers series, Neighborhood Liaison and Community Task Forces, and more."

Contact Ed at everetted@comcast.net.

Finlayson, Roosevelt, and Michael Diggis

Roosevelt and Michael are creating a new framework and practice for organizations called Festival in the Workplace. Inspired by Junkanoo, the name for Carnival in the Bahamas, citizens spend nine months of the year designing and building costumes, creating and practicing music and dance, for parades (they call them "rushes") that take place on Boxing Day and New Year's at midnight.

The festival is wildly creative and all volunteer. It is done with a low budget and tools made out of found objects. It is not just a festival, it is a communal way of being; it helps the community raise its children, it mobilizes and values the gifts of those who otherwise are on the margin.

Roosevelt and Michael embody the values and communal care that Junkanoo stands for. Their effort to bring Festival in the Workplace into organizational life is important, not only for what it can do for a workplace, but also for reminding Bahamians about the culture and tradition that is who they are.

Contact Roosevelt at mdr@coralwave.com.

Freedman, Michael

In their words: "As the Founding Partner of Freedman Tung & Bottomley, Mr. Freedman has become widely known for providing communities with creative and effective solutions to revitalize their downtown districts and regional retail centers, to restructure failing or stagnated commercial corridors and workplace districts, and to create special streets, boulevards, and public places that stimulate new investment and vitality. He specializes in redevelopment and infill master planning, policy writing and in the design of special streets and public places, especially where strategies, plans and designs must be coordinated to achieve successful beneficial change to existing cities."

Freeman Tung & Bottomley Urban Design (www.ftburbandesign.com)

Fry, Harry

Harry is a physician, a cardiologist, who is an agent for transformation. His recent focus is on shifting the relationship between physicians and nurses. He helped initiate a program where nursing and medical students joined for collaborative learning experiences. Small scale, unfunded, under the radar, powerful in its impact on the thinking of the students.

Gallwey, Tim

Tim is a friend and teacher of mine who has revolutionized our thinking about learning. He has a genius for designing learning experiences that create trust in ourselves and cause results in the world. He has eliminated the dividing line between awareness and action. Tim has consistently created powerful programs that seduce us into becoming accountable and effective human beings.

The Inner Game of Work. New York: Random House, 1999.

The Inner Game (www.theinnergame.com)

Heartland Circle

Craig and Patricia Neal, founders, are good friends and teachers of mine.

In their words: "Heartland connects, gathers and convenes leaders who are changing the world through vision in action. Heartland's network and programs serve those called to be our social and organizational pioneers—those who are restoring wholeness to themselves, their organizations, and their communities. Experience the power of one multiplied by the power of many: attend a Thought Leader Gathering, sign up for an Art of Convening Tele-Training, or register for the next VisionHolder Call or Special Program."

Heartland Circle (www.heartlandcircle.com)

Heschel, Abraham Joshua

Quoted in *I Asked for Wonder: A Spiritual Anthology*, edited by Samuel H. Dresner (Crossroad Publishing Co., 1983). (See Part One introduction for quoted passage.)

Hoxsey, Joan and Michael

Joan and Michael are featured in the Findley House story in this book, but they of course are much more than that. They are active in connecting their church to the community through the practice of Appreciative Inquiry. The church is inquiring into its neighbors, working to extend its hospitality, and doing it through convening, small groups, and focusing on possibility.

Relationship Resources LLC (www.relationshipresources.net)

Ihara, Les

Les gives politics a good name. As a state senator in Hawaii, he has made major inroads in creating a more transparent and collaborative state legislature. He is also an important innovator in our thinking about public service and the importance of keeping power in the hands of citizens.

Jacobs, Jane

The Death and Life of Great American Cities. New York: Random House, 2002 (originally published in 1961).

Dark Age Ahead. New York: Random House, 2004.

Healthy Cities, Urban Theory, and Design: The Power of Jane Jacobs (http://bss.sfsu.edu/pamuk/urban/)

Janov, Jill

Jill is an organization development consultant, but that is too small a version of what she does. She has an unerring instinct for collaborative structure and methods. Much of her work is now in the civic and not-for-profit arenas. She also spent considerable time in Africa and has keen insights on the limitations of "aid" and so-called development.

Joyner, Dan

Dan has spent his life in the company of youth and has invested himself in making the six conversations described here his own. He always says yes to an invitation to serve, and shows up with grace and sensitivity.

Kahane, Adam

Solving Tough Problems: An Open Way of Talking, Listening, and Creating New Realities. San Francisco: Berrett-Koehler Publishers, 2004.

Kaufman, Harriet

Every community needs a Harriet. She is the model of a fierce kind of convening leadership. She has been a leader in the collaborative effort between citizens and police, and done this in a peacemaking way. No one keeps their word as diligently as Harriet. She has taught me about the power of convening, for early on she understood that the way we were designing meetings held something special. Harriet is also a very fine sculptor, creating in the graceful form, texture, and space of granite the same qualities that she produces in her commitment to her community.

> *Judaism and Social Justice,* by Harriet Kaufman. Kaufman House Publishers, 1986. (Passage quoted in Chapter 12 is from Shabbat 77b, Babylonian Talmud.)

Keene, Jim

Jim is the best kind of public servant. He has been on the front line of city management for 20 years in Berkeley and Tucson, and now works on a broader landscape as an executive with the leading city managers association. He is also a poet, artist, and intellectual. It is uncommon for someone with these capacities to choose such an activist path in public service. He brings to mind Paolo Freire in Brazil and Nikos Kazantzakis in Greece. Both were artists and educators who spent a part of their career in visible public positions, just the spots most of us avoid. Jim also has maintained his humility, which is why he will most likely deny what I am saying about him here. I have quoted him several times in this book, for he is eager to find new ways of thinking about what makes a difference in the civic arena.

> **International City/County Management Association (www.icma.org)**

Kemp, Clint

There is a large movement of leaders within the Christian church redefining what it means to be Christian in today's society. The leaders of this effort are a group of pastors re-creating what they call the Emergent Church. One of these is Clint Kemp. He is a Bahamian citizen who for many years has been pastor of New Providence Community Center in Nassau. They have created a church that is committed to the environment, to the arts, to social justice, and that has become a center for family life. They have a recreation center and a large greenhouse, and the grounds have become an art gallery. Their programs include all citizens of the Nassau community, regardless of belief systems or denomination.

Clint is also an entrepreneur. He takes people on fly-fishing tours and calls his business Secret Soul. An unusual but compelling form for his ministry.

Secret Soul Fly Fishing Adventures (www.secret-soul.com)

Koestenbaum, Peter

There is no finer consultant and philosopher on earth. Few people of his humanity and intellect have so committed themselves to being useful in the world of business.

In their words: "Philosophy-in-Business™, founded by Peter Koestenbaum, Ph.D., applies the depth and history of *philosophy* to today's bottom line *business* issues in the New Economy for breakthrough results. PiB's goal is to create a 'win-win' in the New Economy by taking a fresh and deep approach to the clash between two imperatives of our time: business results and human values. Philosophy-in-Business goes beyond bland compromises and banal clichés."

> *The Philosophic Consultant: Revolutionizing Organizations with Ideas.* San Francisco: Jossey-Bass, 2003.

> *Freedom and Accountability at Work: Applying Philosophic Insight to the Real World.* San Francisco: Jossey-Bass, 2001.

> *Leadership: The Inner Side of Greatness.* San Francisco: Jossey-Bass, 1991.

> *The Heart of Business: Ethics, Power, and Philosophy.* Dallas: Saybrook, 1987.

> **PiB.net (www.pib.net)**

Korten, David

> *When Corporations Rule the World*, 2nd ed. San Francisco: Berrett-Koehler Publishers, 2001.

The Great Turning: From Empire to Earth Community. San Francisco: Berrett-Koehler Publishers, 2006.

David C. Korten (www.davidkorten.org)

Krippenstapel, Jo

Jo is a consultant and leader in the not-for-profit, or public benefit, world. In a quiet and powerful way, she finds and builds connectedness across the traditional boundaries of community. One result of her connecting has been the creation of an association of public benefit executives. A good part of her work is in the disabilities field and helps this vital segment of our community find its voice and carry the message of inclusiveness for the gifts of all of us. After a recent meeting where Jo agreed to summarize our discussion, she set in poetic stanza form the stream of ideas, dreams, feelings, distractions, and disconnected story lines that are the reality of any gathering. Her expression of the meeting was better than the experience itself. If you want to see these notes, e-mail me. If you want to contact her, a much better choice.

Contact Jo at jokripp@cs.com.

Leonard, Gavin

Gavin, along with others, founded Elementz, which is the most productive space for the affirmation of young urban adults that I have seen. As its executive director, he is the definition of passion, intelligence, and commitment. He invests himself to a fault in the hardest of tasks—the funding, organization, and forward thinking for the city's urban young adults.

See **Elementz.**

Lopez, Barry

Home Ground: Language for an American Landscape, edited by Barry Lopez and Debra Gwartney, with an introduction by Barry Lopez. San Antonio, TX: Trinity University Press, 2006.

Barry Lopez (www.barrylopez.com)

Lukensmeyer, Carolyn

In their words: "AmericaSpeaks, a non-profit organization, engages citizens in the public decisions that impact their lives. It develops innovative deliberative tools that work for both citizens and decision makers. These tools give citizens an opportunity to have a strong voice in public decision making within the increasingly short timeframes required of decision makers. As a result, citizens can impact decisions and those in leadership positions can make more informed, lasting decisions."

> *Public Deliberation: A Manager's Guide to Citizen Engagement,* with Lars Hasselblad Torres. IBM Center for the Business of Government, 2006. Download PDF: http://www.businessofgovernment.org/pdfs/ LukensmeyerReport.pdf.

AmericaSpeaks (www.americaspeaks.org)

Lynch, Damon III

Damon is a courageous and active spokesman for the African-American community in Cincinnati and around the country. After the disturbances and street rebellion in 2001, Damon became a force for organizing a long-term way for the community's response to its outraged youth. He also is an important example of the role the church can play, beyond its boundaries, in creating a more just and compassionate city.

Mailliard, Sadanand Ward and Kranti

Ward and Kranti are changing the face of education. So many of our schools hold to the industrial model of producing adults by teaching values, pouring in information, testing with high stakes, and reducing the arts. Mount Madonna, the school Ward and Kranti have spent decades creating, celebrates the gifts, values, and abilities inherent in each child. They are a living demonstration that, more than pedagogy, instructional design, or curriculum, it is the humanity and love of the teacher that opens a new world for the possibilities of the child.

In their words: "The primary mission of Mount Madonna School is to integrate intellectual, social and creative learning within the context of supportive human relationships. We are dedicated to helping our students become aware of the range of their creative talents and how those talents can be applied in developing a life of positive meaning and purpose."

Mount Madonna School (www.mountmadonnaschool.org)

Project Happiness

In the words of Project Happiness: "Everyone wants to be happy—it's a universal quest. Project Happiness follows a senior high school class from the Mount Madonna School near Watsonville, California, on a journey to discover the true basis of human happiness. Project Happiness reveals a compass to uncover the potential of happiness within. The Mission of Project Happiness is to engage youth in a conversation about how their values and ethics are connected to happiness and to the meaning and purpose in their lives. We often hear Gandhi's quote to 'be the change we want to see in the world.' We want to take this deeper—how can the next generation improve the world around them without dealing with themselves first? Project Happiness is a vehicle for young people from different cultures to recognize that they have the possibility of their own positive transformation within themselves, and it's from this platform that they can directly affect the world around them."

Project Happiness (www.projecthappiness.net)

For reports of their experience:

Project Happiness blog (http://blog.projecthappiness.net/?feed=rss2)

Growing Up in Santa Cruz (http://www.growing-up.com/viewarticle .php?id=127)

Masters, Jane

Jane is an emergent activist who, above all, knows how to honor her word. She is changing the conversation in Cincinnati and is truly a modern alchemist who turns everything she touches to gold. She embodies all that is in this book; no small part of this is through rediscovering her freedom.

Contact Jane at janemasters@cinci.rr.com

McAfee, Barbara

If you believe that the arts are crucial to transformation and social change, Barbara's music fits the bill. She brings her songs and singing into workshops, conferences, and performances in a unique and compelling way. She combines the skill of a therapist with the talent of an artist to engage people in their development. Sometimes we do a presentation or workshop together, and I am always better at what I do because she is doing it with me.

Barbara McAfee (www.barbaramcafee.com)

McCartney, Mike

Mike has given his career to public service at the highest levels, both in elected office and in senior positions in government, the Democratic Party, and the not-for-profit sector. He holds a deep commitment to social justice and keeping public service grounded in the well-being of those on the margins of our communities. At this writing he is president of the Hawaii State Teachers Association.

Hawaii State Teachers Association (www.hsta.org)

McKnight, John

In their words: "The Asset-Based Community Development Institute (ABCD), established in 1995 by the Community Development Program at Northwestern University's Institute for Policy Research, is built upon three decades of community development research by John Kretzmann and John L. McKnight. The ABCD Institute spreads its findings on capacity-building community development in two ways: (1) through extensive and substantial interactions with community builders, and (2) by producing practical resources and tools for community builders to identify, nurture, and mobilize neighborhood assets."

Building Communities from the Inside Out, with John Kretzmann. Center for Urban Affairs, Evanston, IL. Chicago: ACTA Publications, 1994.

Discovering Community Power: A Guide to Mobilizing Local Assets and Your Organization's Capacity, with John Kretzmann. Chicago: ACTA Publications, 2005.

The Careless Society: Community and Its Counterfeits. New York: Basic Books, 1995.

Mapping Community Capacity, with John Kretzmann. Evanston, IL: Center for Urban Affairs and Policy Research, Northwestern University, 1990.

For a complete list of publications, see the Asset-Based Community Development Institute Web site (www.northwestern.edu/ipr/abcd.html).

Miami University Center for Community Engagement

In their words: "The Center establishes collaborations between Miami University and community groups in Over-the-Rhine in order to forge opportunities for student, faculty, and community learning in cross-disciplinary and inter-cultural experiences. The uniqueness of the Center for Community Engagement is its relationship with the Over-the-Rhine People's Movement and other important organizations within the inner city of Cincinnati that struggle for human and racial rights, and social justice. Accordingly, it is a site for learning and for producing knowledge that intersects with the needs and demands of a social movement. The Center privileges human and ecological needs as leading priorities in urban development, and challenges the profit motive as the dominant arbiter in urban social policy."

See Tom Dutton, *above.*

The Miami University Center for Community Engagement in Over-the-Rhine (www.fna.muohio.edu/cce/history.html)

Morris, Barry

Barry is a very experienced organization development consultant. He has for years been generous with his time in the community and has held a number of leadership positions with nonprofit agencies. I always learn when I am with him, and he has developed innovative ways to use the six conversations described in the book in the realm of strategic planning. If you are looking for a consultant, Barry is as good as they get.

Left Lane Consulting (www.leftlaneconsultingllc.com)

Murphy, Ken

Ken has for years been a great friend and partner in my work in organizations. He is also a screenwriter, novelist, and photographer. Why some people get more than their fair share of talent I do not understand.

Contact Ken at kennethmurphy@mac.com.

Murray, Julie

There are certain members of a neighborhood who by nature build relationships. Julie is a master at this. She persistently looks for openings to bring together people who have a long history and story about each other. And if it does not work this time, she just keeps on. Julie has great faith and compassion for people, and also a deep caring for the well-being of all. Amazing human being.

Neumeier, Bonnie

For more than 25 years, Bonnie has lived, fought, loved, and cared for the residents of Over-the-Rhine, a central Cincinnati neighborhood. In the late 1980s, she was instrumental in organizing citizens to purchase a local school building and creating Peaslee Neighborhood Center. This is a place where children, artists, activists, and caring adults can build stronger connectedness to each other and sustain the spirit and soulfulness of this part of the city. Bonnie is also a poet, speaker, and author who has been widely recognized for her commitment and humanity. She recently published the notes and writings of Buddy Gray, an activist and humanitarian who died way too soon.

See **Peaslee Center**, *below.*

Orion Magazine

In their words: "'America's finest environmental magazine' (*Boston Globe*) is an influential forum for re-imagining humanity's relationship to nature, culture, and place, featuring America's foremost writers and artists."

Orion Magazine (www.orionmagazine.org)

Overton, Ann

As executive director of the Mastery Foundation, Ann has brought the ideas of Werner Erhard to those working in the ministry through the Making a Difference workshop. Mastery has also developed a Community Empowerment program, which is having an impact all over the globe. She is one of the most competent and ingenious executives I know. She has assembled a group of volunteers that are as talented, committed, and fun to be with as any I have worked with. If you contact her, ask her about her work on reconciliation in Northern Ireland and Israel. Not the easiest places to create community.

In their words: "The Mastery Foundation is a non-profit, volunteer, interfaith organization established in 1983. The work of the Mastery Foundation is to empower individuals and communities in their ministries, in the reconciliation and healing of divisions, in creating new conversations and possibilities for the future. We are not a foundation in the usual sense of being supported by an endowment. Our financial support comes from individual donors, and almost all our work is done by volunteers—including board members and regular workshop leaders, who pay their own expenses to travel to and lead our programs. We offer programs and initiatives designed to give participants new power and access to what they already know and the ability to bring new possibilities to their current situation."

The Mastery Foundation (www.masteryfoundation.org)

Owen, Harrison

In his words: "Twenty years' experience with Open Space Technology in over 40,000 iterations in 83 countries had demonstrated to myself and thousands of colleagues, that every time space was opened, a most remarkable and unexpected result occurred. I called it Genuine Community, the sort where differences (of opinion, ethnicity, economics, politics etc.) were if anything amplified AND those involved found it possible to treat each other with respect, often coming close to real affection. It seemed to me that another word for this phenomenon is Peace. Furthermore, the deeper the original conflicts, the more intense was the sense of community."

The Practice of Peace, 2nd ed. Circle Pines, MN: Human Systems Dynamics Institute, 2004.

Open Space Technology: A User's Guide, 2nd ed. San Francisco: Berrett-Koehler Publishers, 1997.

The Power of Spirit: How Organizations Transform. San Francisco: Berrett-Koehler Publishers, 2000.

Open Space (www.openspaceworld.com)

Patchett, Ray

Former city manager, Carlsbad, California

Ray is a very special city manager. He has in a unique way applied the ideas of organization development and learning organization to building community. Like no other public servant I know. Several years ago, he, his team, and the city council convened one of the best-designed community conferences I have ever been a part of. His work has been in Carlsbad, California. You can learn more about it from their Web site. Ray is now consulting to other city managers.

See **Carlsbad** *above.*

Contact Ray at Patchettr@aol.com.

Peaslee Neighborhood Center

In their words: "Learning and Growing through Community, Arts and Education. Rooted in the Over-the-Rhine People's Struggle for the right of self-determination, a Seed of HOPE, Peaslee is a place that seeks to welcome and nurture the involvement of neighborhood folk in building a stronger, healthier community where Educational & Cultural & Political Awareness GROW."

Peaslee Neighborhood Center (www.overtherhine.org/peaslee)

Pentz, Doug

Doug has partnered in beginning the Affinity Center, a place where people with addictive and attention challenges can learn how to create a more productive life for themselves. He has been one of the steadfast supporters of A Small Group, our network of people choosing to become engaged in restoring community. As busy and at times consumed as he is with the professional practice he runs, he keeps attending gatherings, occasionally volunteers for projects, but mostly shows up with his gifts of good will, self-awareness, and endearing optimism.

The Affinity Center (www.theaffinitycenter.com)

Public Allies

In their words: "Public Allies advances diverse young leaders to strengthen communities, nonprofits and civic participation. Public Allies has built a powerful model for identifying, training and supporting talented and diverse young adults to lead positive community change. Through our programs, young people, ages 18 to 30, serve in full-time apprenticeships creating, improving and expanding services at local nonprofit organizations, and participate in a rigorous leadership development program that combines weekly training, coaching, team projects and reflection. Public Allies continues to invest in the skills networks and initiatives of our program graduates through a lifetime of structured program, grants, and networking opportunities."

Public Allies (www.publicallies.org)

For Cincinnati: Public Allies, Cincinnati (http://www.publicallies.org/ site/c.liKUL3PNLvF/b.3158715/k.1F41/Cincinnati.htm)

Putnam, Robert D.

In their words: "In *Bowling Alone*, Putnam shows how we have become increasingly disconnected from family, friends, neighbors, and our democratic structures—and how we may reconnect. He warns that our stock of social capital—the very fabric of our connections with each other—has plummeted, impoverishing our lives and communities. *Better Together* provides interactive ways to celebrate and learn from the ways that Americans are connecting, and provides tools and strategies to reconnect with others."

Bowling Alone: The Collapse and Revival of American Community. New York: Simon & Schuster, 2000.

Better Together: Restoring the American Community, with Lewis M. Feldstein. New York: Simon & Schuster, 2003. (Passages quoted in Chapter 1 are from pages 2 to 3.)

Bowling Alone (www.bowlingalone.com)

Better Together (www.bettertogether.org)

Richardson, Bob

Bob is a real estate developer in Sarasota, Florida, who is active as an advocate for a just community. He has sponsored many community-building ventures and has brought his entrepreneurial skill to Goodwill Industries. He was also very generous with his time and talent on a Cincinnati project.

Rogers, Anne

Anne Rogers is committed to bringing the principles of restorative justice to other aspects of the community arena. Her Web site lists links to several programs.

Restorative Solutions (www.restorativesolutions.us)

Rogers, Carl

Carl Rogers' client-centered therapy and its application to teaching has within it elements of a citizen-centered leadership. It is about the authenticity of the therapist/educator and the willingness to structure ways for clients, students, and in our case citizens to take charge of their own learning and futures. The early pages of his book capture the essence of this way of being; the latter pages spell out the practice in education with a great description from a student point of view by Dr. Samuel Tenenbaum, Ph.D. See pages 15–27 and 277–313.

On Becoming a Person. Boston: Houghton Mifflin, 1961.

(SCOPE) Sarasota County Openly Plans for Excellence

In their words: "To engage our community in planning for excellence through a process of open dialogue and impartial research, to establish priorities, propose solutions and monitor change to enhance the quality of life in Sarasota County. SCOPE can help residents learn more about the challenges facing the community and how to connect with the decision-making process to make a difference. Add your voice to new conversations on topics like affordable housing or race and cultural relations. Have a new conversation about the opportunities and possibilities. Why is that so important? Communities whose residents are 'plugged in' and have an increased ownership of the decision-making process are healthier overall. They have lower rates of school dropout, crime, and even fewer colds and heart attacks. So check out SCOPE's community studies and tools. Learn more about where you live. Get connected! It's your community . . . isn't it time you owned it?"

SCOPE (www.scopexcel.org)

Schumacher Society, E. F.

In their words: "The E. F. Schumacher Society, named after the author of *Small Is Beautiful: Economics As If People Mattered,* is an educational non-profit organization founded in 1980. Our programs demonstrate that both social and environmental sustainability can be achieved by applying the values of human-scale communities and respect for the natural environment to economic issues. Building on a rich tradition often known as decentralism, the Society initiates practical measures that lead to community revitalization and further the transition toward an economically and ecologically sustainable society."

The E. F. Schumacher Society (www.smallisbeautiful.org)

Services United for Mothers and Adolescents (SUMA)

In their words: "SUMA (Services United for Mothers and Adolescents) improves the well being and quality of life of children by providing educational, parenting, and preventative services."

SUMA (www.sumaservices.org)

Seven Hills Neighborhood Houses

In their words: "Seven Hills Neighborhood Houses is a community partner dedicated to improving the quality of life of its neighbors through youth education, parent training, employment, micro-enterprise assistance, and senior services."

Seven Hills Neighborhood Houses (www.7hillsnh.org)

Shaffer, Dr. Dorothy P.

In their words: "Full Spectrum Health Center: A healing environment offering exceptional care through concentration on your individual health interests and needs." The Web site has a history and slide show of the renovation of the building and shows pictures of the remodeled interior. Worth a look.

Full Spectrum Health Center (www.full-spectrum.info/index.htm)

Shriberg, Art

Professor of Leadership, Xavier University

CEO, OptimaHR

Art offers training and consulting in leadership. He works in a personal and customized way with his clients. As with any good educator and consultant, who he is as a human being is what makes the difference. He also has a long, generous history of giving to the community. That alone is reason enough to contact him.

In their words: "OptimaHR is dedicated to helping organizations attain maximum returns on their most important investment—their people. We're the same experts that the big firms send in—without the markup or the obstacles. Our difference lies in providing both strategic and operational deliverables that will move your business forward."

OptimaHR (www.optimahr.com)

Smith, Cynthia

Part of her story is in the book. She is assistant director, Client Services, at the Hamilton County Department of Job and Family Services.

Snow, Judith

As mentioned in the book, Judith is a voice for eliminating the distinction called "disabled." If you are looking for a great speaker at a conference or event, get in touch with her.

What's Really Worth Doing and How to Do It: A Book for People Who Love Someone Labeled Disabled. Toronto, ON: Inclusion Press International, n.d.

Inclusion Network: Judith Snow (www.inclusion.com/assnow.html)

Sparough, Geralyn and Tom

Tom is a juggler and Geralyn works in education. The two of them joined Joan and Michael Hoxsey (her parents) in the Findley House story. They have figured out how to bring the intimacy of a family into service to the community. Plus, what is unique about them is that they are extremely independent persons who bring vastly different gifts into the room. The fact that they have kept their differences intact and can still show up in hard places with each other is a rare.

Stec, Jeffrey

Jeff is committed to creating innovative ways to build communities; he guided the example about Covington in the book. He operates within the context of generosity and possibility. He has integrated the ideas on the importance of a new conversation and tied this to strategic planning. He also understands the interaction between relatedness, possibility, and problem solving very well. He is a good one to talk to about how these ideas work in the real world. He calls his business Inspired Community Change, which is what he does.

Jeffrey Stec (www.jeffreystec.com)

Stewart, Steve

Steve is changing the face of journalism and the media. He has used his position as a newspaper publisher to build community, instead of making a living off of the vulnerability of community. When he was publisher in Clarksdale, Mississippi, he convened a series of workshops and conversations to bring the community together, a unique stance for his profession. At this writing, Steve is publisher and president of *The Tidewater News*.

The Tidewater News (www.tidewaternews.com)

Stoeber, Mark

Mark is redefining the role of elected official in Cold Spring, Kentucky. He does his work there in a quiet, effective, relationship-building way, which is a good model for all in public office. He can be found in the mayor's office in Cold Spring, Kentucky.

The Structurist

University of Saskatchewan

In their words, *"The Structurist* is an international art journal, founded in 1960 at the University of Saskatchewan by Eli Bornstein. Incorporating the root word *structure, The Structurist* is concerned with the building processes of creation in art and nature. It focuses upon ideas relating to architecture and the arts—including painting, sculpture, design, photography, music, and literature—their histories and relationships to each other, as well as to science, technology, and nature." (Passage quoted in Welcome is from No. 45/46, 2005/2006, page 2.)

The Structurist (**www.usask.ca/structurist**)

Stuart, Barry D.

Associate, Morris J. Wosk Centre for Dialogue

Adjunct professor, criminology, Simon Fraser University, Vancouver, BC

CSE Consulting Group

In their words: "For the past 35 years, Barry's work has focused on resolving conflicts and improving the decision-making processes in both the public and private sector. He has worked in a wide range of many challenging settings to develop skills and processes to engage conflict in ways that generate innovative solutions and build effective relationships. He is internationally known through his training, teaching, writings and involvement as a mediator, negotiator and facilitator. Barry's principal interest lies in creating safe places for people to engage in the difficult dialogues needed to move through seemingly intractable differences. He has worked in several communities in Canada, the United States and in third world countries to develop community and restorative justice processes as an integral part of enhancing community well-being and sustainability."

Glenn Sigurdson, CSE Group (www.glennsigurdson.com/cse/pro_ relationships.asp)

Sunderland, Steve

There are people in the academic world who care deeply about the larger community and are willing to apply their gifts and intellect to social issues. Steve, a University of Cincinnati professor, is one of those people. He has created the Peace Village, where he brings students into positive contact with others they would never have met otherwise. This is peacemaking at its best.

Peace Village
4129 Georgia Avenue
Cincinnati, OH 45223
E-mail: sundersc@email.uc.edu

Three Square Music Foundation

In their words: "Making a difference in the community, one person at a time." Our events focus on the prevention of drug use and senseless violence in the lives of our youth. We use various tools to accomplish our mission, from various youth interactive programs to live entertainment, we use a variety of tools to reach young people that are looking for something positive out of life."

Three Square Music Foundation (www.threesquaremusic.org)

Toyama, Jimmy

As his story in the text illustrates, Jimmy sees the possibility of a new, community-building politics. Very much needed.

Uhlig, Paul

"Improving Patient Care in Hospitals," *Journal of Innovative Management*, Goal/QPC, Fall 2001.

"System Innovation: Concord Hospital," with others, *The Journal on Quality Improvement*, November 2002.

Urban Opportunities Alliance

In their words: "The Urban Opportunities Alliance is an alliance of independent, community-based organizations that has come together to raise money to expand our ability to empower low-income people in Cincinnati. Through our unique approach, we build relationships through peer-to-peer networks, discover and nurture individuals' gifts, and innovate programs responsive to the needs of the evolving community."

Urban Opportunities Alliance (www.urbanopportunitiesalliance.org)

Weisbord, Marvin

In their words: "Future search is a planning meeting that helps people transform their capability for action very quickly. The meeting is task-focused. It brings together 60 to 80 people in one room or hundreds in parallel rooms. Future search brings people from all walks of life into the same conversation—those with resources, expertise, formal authority and need. They meet for 16 hours spread across three days. People tell stories about their past, present and desired future. Through dialogue they discover their common ground. Only then do they make concrete action plans."

Future Search Network (www.futuresearch.net)

In his words: "After years of answering requests one at a time, I am posting some articles, book excerpts and video clips that I have assembled over the years. This web site identifies people, values, theories, research, and methods related to organization development and social change that I've come to appreciate since 1969."

Marvin Weisbord (www.marvinweisbord.com)

Don't Just Do Something, Stand There! with Sandra Janoff. San Francisco: Berrett-Koehler Publishers, 2007.

Productive Workplaces Revisited: Dignity, Meaning, and Community in the 21st Century. San Francisco: Jossey-Bass/Wiley, 2004.

Future Search: An Action Guide to Finding Common Ground in Organizations and Communities, with Sandra Janoff, 2nd ed. San Francisco: Berrett-Koehler Publishers, 2000.

Discovering Common Ground, with 35 International Authors. San Francisco: Berrett-Koehler Publishers, 1992.

Productive Workplaces: Organizing and Managing for Dignity, Meaning, and Community. San Francisco: Jossey-Bass, 1987.

White, Byron

Byron has brought the asset-based work of McKnight to Xavier University and the Cincinnati community. He is providing a strong link to the grassroots people in Xavier's neighborhood. This is unfortunately rather unique among most higher-education institutions. Byron is associate vice president of the Community Building Collaborative at Xavier; Liz Blume is executive director of the Community Building Institute.

In their words: "The Community Building Institute facilitates collaborative action among residents, local organizations and institutions that leads to comprehensive, asset-based community development."

Community Building Institute (www.xavier.edu/communitybuilding)

Yes! Magazine

In their words: "Supporting you in creating a more just, sustainable and compassionate world."

Yes! (www.yesmagazine.org)

Zakaria, Fareed

The Future of Freedom: Illiberal Democracy at Home and Abroad, rev. ed. New York: W. W. Norton, 2007.

Acknowledgments

Bob Havlick, then head of the Innovation Groups, a forward-thinking association of city managers, got me involved in communities. He kept inviting me to their annual conference, and my contact with these public servants shifted the direction of my work. I will always be grateful for Bob's faith and support. Work with some of those city managers, Jim Keene, Jim Ley, Ray Patchett, and Ed Everett, sealed the deal, and I am grateful to all of them.

My gratitude to Peter Koestenbaum, John McKnight, and Werner Erhard is infinite. I keep looking for sentences I speak or write that have not been shaped by their friendship, and I can find few. I do not know if I have a thought that is truly my own, so I am happily relegated to the role of translator and secondary source for their insights.

Others who have given support to these ideas are Tom DiBello and Jim Tucker. They have invited me into places that were challenging and confirming, so I thank them both.

Bernard Booms thinks he has been the beneficiary of my work, but the opposite is true. Bernard teaches me generosity with each call. Plus he is an economist and a marketing professor who has both sustained and transcended his training to bring humanity and care into his work. Special and rare.

Art Shriberg is a friend and professor of leadership in Xavier University's business school, but more important, he brings an unerring warmth and commitment to his community. He created an invitation for me to be a guest consultant to Xavier, and it is always a pleasure to work with his students.

He is also a great consultant to organizations. Cincinnati is a better place because he is in it.

There are certain friends who are constant and always interested. Michael Johnston is an expert on living with integrity, playful when not working, and the best coach on the planet.

Much of my work in Cincinnati is sustained by the passion and emotional intelligence of Collette Thompson. She complements me in that she remembers people's names, actually is energized by being with people, and gets upset for the right reasons; and when something on the ground needs to get done, she always does it. Always.

Leslie Stephen has been my editor for all but one of the books I have written. She is a beautiful advocate for the reader, has a genius for structure, and is profoundly interested in ideas and how they change the world. Above all, she cares about keeping my voice intact, as ungrammatical as it is. I would stop writing if Leslie were not in the picture.

Steve Piersanti is a dream of a publisher. He has created an independent publishing company that lives out the ideas contained in what he publishes. Steve is a person of enduring faith and has the gift of editing that I pay attention to, even when I am not listening.

A book is also given life by its reviewers. I want to thank Frank Basler, Jeff Kulick, Ann Matranga, Elianne Obadia, and Joseph A. Webb, for they each put energy, far beyond any compensation for the task, into understanding and caring about the quality of the book. I am also grateful to Elissa Rabellino, who performed the copyediting for the book. She gave great attention to the manuscript and was a fine advocate for the reader. Elissa is really good at what she does.

Thanks also to Cliff Bolster and Bill Brewer, who read an early manuscript and were generous with their thoughts. Allan Cohen and Ann Overton have been central to the ideas in this book. Their friendship is sustaining, and their way of thinking and being is so convergent with mine that when I am in a difficult situation I often think that they would do a better job than I.

I have dedicated this book to Maggie Rogers, but to fully acknowledge what she has given to the creation of it and all else I do would require a separate book in itself. Enough here to say thank you again.

Finally, I want to express gratitude to my family. Thanks to Jim, my brother, a kind soul who has generously offered his genius as a photographer to all of us; he deserves special thanks for enduring me as a subject. He offered to airbrush my last photo and next time I will take him up on it. My daughters, Jennifer and Heather, who, through their love, have given me a reason to live a decent life. My grandchildren, Leyland, Gracie, and Auggie are beautiful beyond the natural pride of a grandfather. They give me reason to live a long time. Finally, I want to express my love for Cathy, David, and Ellen. Every day they keep me on my toes and engaged in a future. With them I am learning the value of surrender, of acceptance, and about the soft and tender fabric that lies within all of us. In return, they put up with me, so who could ask for anything more?

Index

A

accountability, 24, 30, 63
  choosing, 21
  and commitment, 71–72
  and communal possibility, 48
  creating a community of, 98
  and entitlement, 70–71
  weakness in dominant view of, 71
action, expanded notion of, 80–81
advice-free zone, creating, 109–110
Affinity Center, 213
Alban, Billie, 12, 22, 191
Alexander, Christopher, 12, 18–20, 30,
    47, 83, 158, 187–188
  aliveness/wholeness, 19
  transformation as unfolding, 19–20
aliveness, 19, 30–31, 178
  bring to the physical space, 153–155
Allah, Islord, 188
alternative future, 87, 178
ambiguous questions, 106
AmericaSpeaks, 206
anxiety-evoking questions, 106
anxiety of invitation, 115
apartness, 2
art collections, on walls, 157

Art of Hosting and Convening Conver-
    sations, 188
Asset-Based Community Development
    movement, 13
Asset-Based Community Development
    Institute (ABCD), 208–209
associational life, 13–14, 30–31
  devaluing, 43–44
auditoriums, 152
Axelrod, Dick and Emily, 12, 22, 189

B

belonging, 79
  absence of, 1–2
  alchemy of, 83–84
  filling the need for, 2–3
  and large groups, 31
  structure of, 4
benchmarking, 77
Better Together (Putnam/Feldstein),
    17–18, 214
Blackonomics, 168, 193
bonding social capital, 18
Bornstein, David, 12, 25–26, 74, 114–
    115, 190
  Cohen's emergent design, 26–27

combining insights, 27–28
small scale/slow growth, 25–26
Bowling Alone (Putnam), 5–6, 17, 214
brainstorming, 77
breakdown of community, 34
Brewer, Bill, 195
Breyfogle, Gina, 79
bridging social capital, 18
Brook, Peter, 67, 190
Brown, Juanita, 12, 97, 190
Brundage, Theresa, 191
Bunker, Barbara, 12, 22, 191
Burke, Tricia, 49–51, 191
Butler, Mike, 132, 191–192

C
cafeterias, 153
Cage, John, 67
Carlsbad, California (example), 146, 192
Casarez, Margaret, 192
Cass, Phil, 110, 192
cause, inversion of, 65–66
Center for Community Engagement
    (Cincinnati, Ohio), 196–197
Center for Great Neighborhoods of
    Covington, Kentucky, 194
chair selection, 155
Cincinnati (Ohio) Public Schools, 193
citizen-driven design, 159–162
Citizens on Patrol, 166
citizenship, 63–72
    defined, 65
    meaning of, 64–65
classrooms, 152–153
Clermont Counseling Center, 49–51,
    191
clients, 63–64
Clingman, James, 168, 193
cocreation, 11, 104, 105, 128

Cohen, Allan, 12, 26–27, 193
Cold Spring, Kentucky (example), 91
collaborative care, 172–174
collective change, 75
Columbus (Ohio) Medical Association
    and Foundation, 192
commerce, using the language of, 44
commitment, 181
    and accountability, 71–72
    defined, 72
    "no" as the beginning of, 132–133
    promises embraced by, 137
commitment conversation, 124, 136–
    139, 183–184
    and lip service, 136–137
    questions for, 137–139
communal possibility, 48
communal teaching stories, 35
communal transformation, 60, 76
    initiation of, 93–94
    and leadership, 85–92
community, 6
    breakdown of, 34
    as conversation, 52–53
    economic prosperity of, 43
    as problems to be solved, 32–33
    reconciliation of, 163
    shifting the context for, 29–36
    social capital, 5
    social fabric of, 9–10
    stuck, 37–46
    symptoms, limitations of, 33–34
    trading problems for possibilities, 4
    transformation of, 1–7
community building:
    complexity of, 9–10, 78–80
    and leadership, 86
Community Building Institute, 222
community policing, 191–192

community transformation, 73–81

compassion, marginalization in public conversation, 44

conference rooms, 152

consumers, 63–64

context:

compared to culture, 56

defined, 29

dominant, 32–33

power of, 15

principles of strategy, 30–32

and questions, 103–104

convener, 68, 87–88, 120, 128, 136–137, 153

convening, art of, 88–90

conversation, 98–99, 178

advice-free zone, creating, 109–110

community as, 52–53

questions, 101–110

use of term, 32

Cooper Reed, Eileen, 193

Cornerstone Community Loan Fund, 193–194

Covington, Kentucky (example):

Center for Great Neighborhoods, 194

transformation in, 79–80

Covrett, Donna, 194

culture, compared to context, 56

Cunningham, Ken, 159–162, 194

cynicism, 42, 117

ultimate cost of, 71–72

D

Dannemiller, Kathie, 12, 22–23, 118–119, 195

denial, 133–134

depth, choosing over speed, 75–76

design, and cost/speed, 162

Designed Learning, 195–196

destination strategy, 76–77

development:

and the local economy, 167–168

and reconciliation, 168

dialogue, 15, 19, 22, 53, 99, 106, 155, 156, 215, 219, 221

DiBello, Tom, 79

Diggis, Michael, 199–200

dissent, 181

creating space for, 130

and doubt, 131–133

as a form of refusal, 135

dissent conversation, 124, 130–136, 182–183

denial, 133–134

distinctions for, 133–135

"no" as the beginning of commitment, 132–133

questions for, 135–136

rebellion, 134

resignation, 134

Don't Just Do Something, Stand There! (Weisbord/Janoff), 119

doubt, and dissent, 131–133

Dutton, Tim, 196

Dutton, Tom, 196–197

E

E. F. Schumacher Society, 215–216

economic prosperity, and job creation, 43

elected officials, convening capacity of, 90–92

Elementz, 60–61, 188, 197, 205

emergent design, 26–27

Emory, Fred and Marilyn, 22

engagement, 87, 178

and large group methodologies, 25

entitlement, 70–71
  and accountability, 70–71
  cost of, 70
Erhard, Werner, 12, 14–17, 27, 197–198, 211
  power of context, 15
  power of language, 14–15
  power of possibility, 15–17
Erpenbeck, Joe, 198
Everett, Ed, 198

F
faith, 42
family well-being, and human services, 169–170
fault marketing, 38–39, 55–56
fear-cycle, 53–56
  payoffs from, 57
fear, marketing, 37–39, 55–56
Festival in the Workplace, 199–200
Findley House, 89–90
Finlayson, Roosevelt, 199–200
Fossett, Jay, 79
fragmentation, effects of, 2–3
fragmented community, transformation of, 1–7
framing the choice, 120
Freedman, Michael, 159, 200
freedom, choosing, 21
Freeman Tung & Bottomley Urban Design, 200
Freire, Paolo, 109, 203
Fry, Harry, 200
Full Spectrum Health Center, 216
Future of Freedom, The (Zakaria), 64
Future Search, 22, 221

G
Gallwey, Tim, 200–201

gathering, use of term, 86
gifts, 181
  focusing on, 12–13, 177
gifts conversation, 124, 139–143, 184
  core questions, 142
  distinctions for, 139–140
  gift-each-brings-to-the-world question, 142
  gifts-of-this-gathering question, 140–141
  questions for, 140
Go Cincinnati, 44
goals, establishing, 77
Grameen Bank, 27–28

H
hallways, 153
Hamilton County Department of Job and Family Services, 170–171, 198
Hawaii State Teachers Association, 208
Hawaiian Democratic Party, 97–98
health care, 171–172
Heartland Circle, 201
helplessness, ultimate cost of, 71–72
Heschel, Abraham Joshua, 9, 201
Hlatshway, Godwin, 103–104
hospitality, 145–149
  breaking bread together, 148–149
  connecting questions, 146–147
  early departure, 147–148
  invitation, restating, 146
  late arrivals, 147
  and the restorative community, 114
  welcome/greeting, 145–146
Hosseini, Khaled, 46
How to Change the World (Bornstein), 12, 190

Hoxsey, Joan and Michael, 89–90, 166, 201
human services, and family well-being, 169–170

I

Ihara, Les, 43, 202
implementation, 77
Inclusion Network, 217
individual changes, aggregation of, 74
International City/County Management Association, 203
inversion of cause:
  and accountability, 179
  utility of, 67–69
invitation, 113–122, 180
  anxiety of, 115
  authentic, 114
  commitment to, as core strategy, 117
  elements of, 119
  framing the choice, 120
  as a language act, 118
  list, 118–119
  making it personal, 122
  naming the hurdle, 121–122
  naming the possibility, 119–120
  radical aspect of, 116–117
  reinforcing the request, 122
  as a request, 118
  restating, 146
  risks of, 115
  as a way of being, 117–118
invitation conversation, distinction for, 114–115
Isaacs, David, 86, 97, 190
isolation, 1–2
  reinforcing, 45

J

Jacobs, Jane, 52–53, 167, 202
Janoff, Sandra, 22, 119
Janov, Jill, 202
job creation, and economic prosperity, 43
Joyner, Dan, 202

K

Kahane, Adam, 35, 202
Kaufman, Harriet, 120, 203
Kazantzakis, Nikos, 203
Keene, Jim, 6, 203
Kemp, Clint, 203–204
Koestenbaum, Peter, 12, 20–21, 66, 204
  freedom/accountability, 21
  paradox, appreciating, 20–21
Korten, David, 43, 204–205
Kretzmann, Jody, 14
Krippenstapel, Jo, 205

L

labeling, 59–60
Landmark Education, 197–198
language, power of, 14–15
large group interventions, 97
large group methodologies, 21–25
  accountability/commitment, 24
  bias toward the future, 25
  conference model, 22
  engagement, importance of, 25
  Future Search, 22
  key insights of, 23–25
  learning from one another, 24
  whole-scale change, 22–23
  World Café method, 23
large groups:
  and belonging, 31
  role of, 96–98

large-scale transformation, 93
laws/oversight, ramping up, 39–40
leaders, role of, 74–75
leadership, 85–92, 179
  convening, art of, 88–90
  elected officials, convening capacity of, 90–92
  romanticizing, 40–41
Leonard, Gavin, 205
Liliuokalani (queen of Hawaii), 83
limiting stories, 35
lip service, and commitment, 136–137
local government, responsibilities of, 91–92
Longmont, Colorado, police department, 191–192
Lopez, Barry, 33–34, 205
Lukensmeyer, Carolyn, 12, 22, 206
Lynch, Damon III, 206

M

Mailliard, Sadanand Ward and Kranti, 206–207
marketing of fear, 37–39
Masters, Jane, 207
Mastery Foundation, 211
McAfee, Barbara, 208
McCartney, Mike, 97–98, 208
McKnight, John, 12–14, 43, 59, 63, 78, 134, 208–209
  Asset-Based Community Development, 13
  associational life, 13–14
  citizen's identification/solving of problems, 14
  gifts, focusing on, 12–13
Media, 46
Miami University Center for Community Engagement, 209

midterm review, 111–112
Morris, Barry, 209–210
Mother Teresa, 72
Mount Madonna School, 206–207
movable chairs, 155
Moyers, Bill, 38
Murphy, Ken, 116–117, 210
Murray, Julie, 210

N

Nature of Order, Book 1: The Phenomenon of Life (Alexander), 18, 158
needs:
  analyzing, 77
  identifying, 76
Neighbor Watch, 166
networks, value of, 75
Neumeier, Bonnie, 210
Northcliffe, Lord, 46
not for profits, 44

O

On Becoming a Person (Rogers), 215
Open Space Technology, 211–212
opportunities, designing/building, 158–162
OptimaHR, 216–217
Orion magazine, 211
Overton, Ann, 193, 211
Owen, Harrison, 22, 211–212
ownership, 181
  defined, 128
ownership conversation, 123, 127–130, 181–182
  confronting stories, 130
  distinctions for, 128
  early questions, 129
  guilt question, 129

indifference, as denial of ownership, 127
innocence, as denial of ownership,
127
story questions, 130

P

paradox, appreciating, 20–21
Patchett, Ray, 145–146, 192, 212
Peaslee Neighborhood Center, 210,
212–213
Pentz, Doug, 213
personal questions, 106
Philosophy-Business (PiB), 204
Phoenix Place, 49–51, 192
physical space:
amplifying, 154–155
arranging as the shape of things
to come, 154
auditoriums, 152
bringing aliveness to, 153–155
bringing art/aesthetic into, 156–157
cafeterias, 153
chairs in, 155
classrooms, 152–153
conference rooms, 152
designing to support community,
151–162, 184–185
hallways, 153
picking a room with a view, 154
platform/stage, 155–156
reception areas, 153
walls, 157
welcoming nature into, 154
platform/stage, 155–156
political suffering, 164–165
possibility, 181
marginalizing, 42–43
power of, 15–17

possibility conversation, 123, 124–125,
181
distinctions for, 125–126
questions for, 126–127
problem solving, 76–80
steps in, 76–77
Project Happiness, 207
projection, 57–59
and labeling, 59–60
taking back, 60
protest, 134
Public Allies, 213
public benefit sector, 44
public safety, 166–167
Putnam, Robert D., 5–6, 12, 17–18, 28,
78, 214

Q

questions, 101–110, 177, 180, 181
ambiguous, 106
anxiety-evoking, 106
construction of, 103–104
for dissent conversation, 135–136
distinctions, 108
with great power, 105–107
with little power, 104–105
personal, 106
for possibility conversation, 126–127
risk order of, 110
setup, 107
unpopular answers, giving permission for, 108–109

R

raised platform, 156
rebellion, and dissent, 134
reception areas, 153
reconciliation, and development, 168
relatedness, choosing over scale, 75–76

Relationship Resources LLC, 201
resignation, and dissent, 134
restoration, 34–36
    and aliveness/wholeness, 47
    essential aspect of, 48
    steps to, 52
restorative community, 47–54, 178
    community as conversation, 52–53
    creation of, 48
    and hospitality, 114
    shifting the context from retribu-
        tive community to, 53–55
restorative justice movement, 51–52
retribution, 42
    context of, 53–56
retributive context of, 45
return on social investment, 44
Richardson, Bob, 214
risk order of questions, 110
Robert's Rules of Order, 94
Rogers, Anne, 214
Rogers, Carl, 215
romanticized leadership, 40–41

S
safety meetings, 166–167
Sarasota County Openly Plans for
    Excellence), 196, 215
scale, 74
    choosing relatedness over, 75–76
Schumacher, E. F., 215–216
Schurch, Carole, 40
Secret Soul Fly Fishing Adventures, 204
self-interest, 37, 47
    reinforcing, 45
Services United for Mothers and Ado-
    lescents (SUMA), 216
Seven Hills neighborhood center,
    Cincinnati, Ohio, 89–90, 216

Shaffer, Dr. Dorothy P., 174–175, 216
Shriberg, Art, 216–217
Small Group, A (ASG), 189, 213
small groups, 178, 179–180
    power of, 95–96
    as unit of transformation, 31, 93–99
Smith, Cynthia, 170–171, 217
Snow, Judith, 139–140, 217
Sobonfu, 143
social capital, 5
    bonding/bridging, 18
social fabric, 177
    building, 30
    of community, 9–10
    creation of, 11
Solving Tough Problems (Kahane), 35
Sparough, Geralyn and Tom, 89–90,
    166, 217
speed, 74
    choosing depth over, 75–76
Spencer, John, 159–162, 194
stage, 155–156
Stec, Jeff, 79, 218
Stewart, Steve, 218
Stoeber, Mark, 91, 218
storytelling, 34–36
Structurist, The, 218–219
Stuart, Barry D., 51, 219
stuck community, 37–46
    associational life, devaluing, 43–44
    fear, marketing of, 37–39
    laws/oversight, ramping up of,
        39–40
    media, 46
    political agenda, 40
    possibility, marginalizing, 42–43
    romanticized leadership, 40–41
    self-interest/isolation, reinforcing,
        45

SUMA (Services United for Mothers and Adolescents), 216
Sunderland, Steve, 219–220
swivel chairs, 155
symptoms, limitations of, 33–34

T

Three Square Music Foundation, 220
Tidewater News, The, 218
Toyama, Jimmy, 97–98, 220
transformation, 1–7
    insights into, 11
    key to, 10
    linguistic nature of, 31, 74
    need for, 6–7
    as unfolding, 19–20
transforming community, 73–81
Truth and Reconciliation Commission, South Africa, 52

U

Uhlig, Paul, 172–174, 175, 220
unfolding, transformation as, 19–20
Urban Opportunities Alliance, 220

V

vision, creating, 78

W

walls, decorating, 157
Weisbord, Marvin, 12, 22, 119, 221
White, Byron, 221–222
whole-scale change, 22–23
Whole-Scale Change: Unleashing the Magic in Organizations (Dannemiller), 195
wholeness, 19
Whyte, William H., 157
Women of Worth, 50–51
World Café, 23, 86, 190
worldview, 29–31

Y

Yes! magazine, 222
youth, 165–166
Yunus, Muhammad, 27

Z

Zakaria, Fareed, 64, 222

About the Author

Peter Block is an author, consultant, and citizen of Cincinnati, Ohio. His work is about empowerment, stewardship, chosen accountability, and the reconciliation of community.

Peter is the author of several best-selling books. The most widely known being *Flawless Consulting: A Guide to Getting Your Expertise Used*, rev. ed. (Jossey-Bass/Pfeiffer, 1998); *Stewardship: Choosing Service Over Self-Interest* (Berrett-Koehler Publishers, 1993), and *The Empowered Manager: Positive Political Skills at Work* (Jossey-Bass, 1987).

He has also authored *The Flawless Consulting Fieldbook and Companion: A Guide to Understanding Your Expertise* (Jossey-Bass/Pfeiffer, 2000), assisted by Andrea Markowitz; and *The Answer to How Is Yes: Acting on What Matters* (Berrett-Koehler Publishers, 2002), which won the 2002 Independent Publisher Book Award for Business Breakthrough Book of the Year. *Freedom and Accountability at Work: Applying Philosophic Insight to the Real World* was coauthored with consultant and philosopher Peter Koestenbaum (Jossey-Bass/Pfeiffer, 2001).

The books are about ways to create workplaces and communities that work for all.

He is a partner in Designed Learning, a training company he founded that offers workshops that build on the skills outlined in his books. If you would like to learn more about these workshops, contact Designed Learning at 866-770-2227 or visit www.designedlearning.com.

Peter serves on the boards of directors of Cincinnati Public Radio; Elementz: Hip Hop Youth Arts Center; and InkTank, which offers writing programs for marginalized people. He is also a partner in the Urban Opportunities Alliance, a group of youth- and family-oriented efforts in Cincinnati. He is a member of the advisory board for the Festival in the Workplace Institute, Bahamas. With other volunteers, Peter began A Small Group, whose work is to bring the disengaged into community through the tools of civic engagement.

Peter's office is in Mystic, Connecticut. You can visit his Web sites at www.peterblock.com, www.designedlearning.com, and www.asmallgroup.net. He welcomes being contacted at pbi@att.net.

About the Design

I believe that the design and feel of a book is as important as its content. There are too many books where I have had to fight the type and interior design in order to extract the content. Small type, crowded pages, no white space, invasive footnotes, no transitions or breathing spaces. These visual qualities in a book neglect the experience of the reader. As if the reader was not important, only the ideas. Leigh McLellan has given her life and talent to book design. She has created a very elegant form for this book and I invited her to comment on the thinking behind her creation:

> The title of the book, *Community: The Structure of Belonging*, suggests both structure and accessibility, a concept enhanced by Peter's open, conversational style. Also, Peter was concerned with judicious use of white space in the design.
>
> The feeling of structure is expressed by the rules (horizontal lines) placed on the part and chapter openings, giving shape to the beginning of each section. On the chapter opening pages, I indented the first lines of the introductory paragraphs to give the reader a little door of white space into the text, an invitation to enter. This indent also creates a more open, informal appearance. To further this and to lend a touch of elegance, I also added space between the letters in the titles and headings.
>
> Quotes are contained in boxes at the edge of the text to lend interest to the page and to give the eye an occasional rest. They also pull the eye outward, momentarily expanding the reading area.
>
> For the text type, I chose a crisp, contemporary face, aptly named Utopia. I complimented the squarishnes of the letter shapes with Tiepolo Bold for the titles, and selected sans serif Frutiger for contrast

in handling the different kinds of text in the book, especially the introductory paragraph and the Example text. The title and halftitle pages are set with Frutiger capitals as a lead-in from the san serif cover type. The large dot on both pages reflects the circular cover motif.

Book design in sum: structure, elegance, consistency, an organic whole in which every part pulls and pushes every other part with both tension and harmony. Each element must be distinct yet recognizably related. Interconnected, like members of a community, as Peter so beautifully expressed in his Welcome.

—*Leigh McLellan*

DATE DUE

About
Berrett-Koehler Publishers

Berrett-Koehler is an independent publisher dedicated to an ambitious mission: Creating a World That Works for All.

We believe that to truly create a better world, action is needed at all levels—individual, organizational, and societal. At the individual level, our publications help people align their lives with their values and with their aspirations for a better world. At the organizational level, our publications promote progressive leadership and management practices, socially responsible approaches to business, and humane and effective organizations. At the societal level, our publications advance social and economic justice, shared prosperity, sustainability, and new solutions to national and global issues.

A major theme of our publications is "Opening Up New Space." They challenge conventional thinking, introduce new ideas, and foster positive change. Their common quest is changing the underlying beliefs, mindsets, institutions, and structures that keep generating the same cycles of problems, no matter who our leaders are or what improvement programs we adopt.

We strive to practice what we preach—to operate our publishing company in line with the ideas in our books. At the core of our approach is *stewardship*, which we define as a deep sense of responsibility to administer the company for the benefit of all of our "stakeholder" groups: authors, customers, employees, investors, service providers, and the communities and environment around us.

We are grateful to the thousands of readers, authors, and other friends of the company who consider themselves to be part of the "BK Community." We hope that you, too, will join us in our mission.

Be Connected

Visit Our Website

Go to www.bkconnection.com to read exclusive previews and excerpts of new books, find detailed information on all Berrett-Koehler titles and authors, browse subject-area libraries of books, and get special discounts.

Subscribe to Our Free E-Newsletter

Be the first to hear about new publications, special discount offers, exclusive articles, news about bestsellers, and more! Get on the list for our free e-newsletter by going to www.bkconnection.com.

Get Quantity Discounts

Berrett-Koehler books are available at quantity discounts for orders of ten or more copies. Please call us toll-free at (800) 929-2929 or email us at bkp.orders@aidcvt.com.

Host a Reading Group

For tips on how to form and carry on a book reading group in your workplace or community, see our website at www.bkconnection.com.

Join the BK Community

Thousands of readers of our books have become part of the "BK Community" by participating in events featuring our authors, reviewing draft manuscripts of forthcoming books, spreading the word about their favorite books, and supporting our publishing program in other ways. If you would like to join the BK Community, please contact us at bkcommunity@bkpub.com.